National Narratives of Mali

National Narratives of Mali

Fula Communities in Times of Crisis

Dougoukolo Alpha Oumar Ba Konaré

LEXINGTON BOOKS
Lanham • Boulder • New York • London

Published by Lexington Books
An imprint of The Rowman & Littlefield Publishing Group, Inc.
4501 Forbes Boulevard, Suite 200, Lanham, Maryland 20706
www.rowman.com

6 Tinworth Street, London SE11 5AL, United Kingdom

Copyright © 2021 by The Rowman & Littlefield Publishing Group, Inc.

All rights reserved. No part of this book may be reproduced in any form or by any electronic or mechanical means, including information storage and retrieval systems, without written permission from the publisher, except by a reviewer who may quote passages in a review.

British Library Cataloguing in Publication Information Available

Library of Congress Cataloging-in-Publication Data

Names: Oumar Ba Konaré, Dougoukolo Alpha, author.
Title: National narratives of Mali : Fula communities in times of crisis / Dougoukolo Alpha Oumar Ba Konaré.
Description: Lanham, Maryland : Lexington Books, 2021. | Includes bibliographical references and index.
Identifiers: LCCN 2020055074 (print) | LCCN 2020055075 (ebook) | ISBN 9781793602657 (cloth) | ISBN 9781793602664 (epub)
Subjects: LCSH: Fula (African people)—Mali—Ethnic identity. | Fula (African people)—Mali—Social conditions. | Identity (Psychology)—Mali. | Mali—Politics and government—21st century. | Mali—Ethnic relations.
Classification: LCC DT551.45.F85 O96 2021 (print) | LCC DT551.45.F85 (ebook) | DDC 305.896322—dc23
LC record available at https://lccn.loc.gov/2020055074
LC ebook record available at https://lccn.loc.gov/2020055075

Dedication
To my paternal grandmothers, Cherif the Bamanan, and Bintily the Fula, because our narrative is made of many stories, as are our lines.

Contents

Acknowledgments	ix
Linguistic Note	xi
Acronyms	xiii
Introduction	1
1 Theoretical Framing of Narratives and Stereotypes	11
2 Narrating Mali and Malians	19
3 Birthing and Updating Narratives	31
4 Clashing Episodes in Fula Narratives	47
5 Looking toward Lasting Paradigms	63
Conclusion	91
References	97
Index	103
About the Author	105

Acknowledgments

We would like to thank all our colleagues in the field, ever-enduring and passionate about human rights. We hope the future brings about more hope than these dreary years. We have strived to make understandable the previous experiences we have shared.

We are very grateful for our researcher colleagues as well for all the conversations, exchanges of data and tools, namely Ousmane Aly Diallo, Racky Ka, Sadio Soukouna, Niandou Touré, and Laure Traoré.

Finally, many thanks to our family: Adame Ba, Safiatou Ba, Alpha Oumar Konaré, Kadiatou Konaré, Mamadou Lamine Konaré, Birama Konaré, Binta Sylla, Alpha Oumar Junior Konaré. They have been there with constant support, even as we have kept discarding attachment to pragmatic needs in order to focus on learning, and advocacy, and teaching. This has been quite a privilege. You have accomplished all this. Please, be proud.

Linguistic Note

Words in West African languages are transcribed using usage conventions in these languages. Below are some keys to help them read when the pronunciation of the letters differs from French. Otherwise, the pronunciation of the letters is identical to French.

The following letters have special pronunciations for English speakers.

ɓ: Its bilabial implosive.
ɗ: Its alveolar implosive.
ƴ: Its palatal implosive.

These three sounds and letters do not exist in English nor in French, nor in Bamanan. In this work, they are specific to the Pulaar language.

c: Pronounced "tch," as in the English word "chalk."
g: Pronounced as in the "big."
h: Pronounced "h" as in "heights."
j: Pronounced "dj," as in "joke."
e: Pronounced "è," as in the name "Ben."
u: Pronounced as in "mood."

All letters are individually pronounced. For example, both "o" in the word "laana," or both "g" in the word "doggude."

Acronyms

AOF	French Occidental Africa
AQIM	Al-Qaida in the Islamic Maghreb
CMFPR	Coordination of Movements and Patriotic Resistance Front
DDR	Demobilization, disarmament, and reintegration
DRC	Democratic Republic of the Congo
ECOWAS	The Economic Community of West African States
FAMA	Malian Armed Forces
GATIA	Self-Defense Group of Imghad Tamasheq and Allies
GBG	Gender-Based Violence
HCUA	High Council for the Unity of Azawad
IDP	Internally displaced person
IHL	International humanitarian law
ISGS	Islamic State in the Greater Sahara
JNIM	Group for the Support of Islam and Muslims
MAA	Arab Movement of Azawad.
MIShal	African Union Mission for Mali and the Sahel
MDP	Movement for the Defense of the Fatherland
MINUSMA	United Nations Multidimensional Integrated Stabilization Mission in Mali
MNLA	National Movement for the Liberation of Azawad
MSA	Movement for the Salvation of Azawad
MUJWA	Movement for Oneness and Jihad in West Africa
UNESCO	United Nations Education, Science, and Culture Organization

Introduction

Mali is currently one of those countries that have been requiring attention from the international community. The Organization of the United Nations has voted resolution 2100 under Chapter VII pertaining to "action with respect to threats to peace, breaches to the peace, and acts of aggression,"[1] so that the international community could join forces in order to not only protect the country but also ensure that stability could be built, so as to enable peace and prosperity in a fragile Sahel-Sahara area.

From 2012, Mali has been talked about with regards to fundamentalist Islamic armed groups and rebels vying for more identity-related rights such as Tamasheq rebels. Both types of movements are deemed as insurgents.

There is, however, a clear divide in all narratives that support a binary view of non-state armed groups. On the one hand, media and political narratives posit that Jihadist movements are terrorist groups. Such characterization comes with classifications and modes of engagement proper to the trope of the "war on terror," with a focus on confrontation and complete military victory. On the other hand, irredentist and self-defense groups, however noxious or powerful, are met with far more complacency, both at a local level and at an international level. Ethnic cleansing and mass murders were met with tepid reactions even as the massacre of Ogossagou happened on March 23, 2019.[2]

Narratives of identity conflicts have been varying, and each of them brings a set of values, of rules of engagement, of friction in local and international doctrines, because agendas of interactions vary based on the classification of each group. Just as these narratives are envisioned outside of armed groups, so are they also created, manipulated, and imposed by armed groups in order to justify their stances, to make statements, to negotiate in power plays. These narratives may become sacrosanct visions of relationships between stakeholders. As such, they appear as variables of warmongering, but also as purported tools for peacebuilding. That may be problematic when it is solely assumed that, de facto, peace and survival rest on subjective appropriation of notions on self and group identity, rather than on evidence-based items that may be summoned and ideally point to clear-cut strategies. That ideal situation does not exist.

This work is not a critique of values-based political and military actions. Rather, it is a critical description of subjective elements put together to push for greater political and geostrategic agendas in the context of Mali, with the situation of the Fula people between 2012 and 2018, as a monographic case. Identity cannot be dissociated from conflict, even when other variables are at play[3] (governance, security, justice, etc.).

Narratives have been at least as esteemed as more evidence-based approaches. Narratives used by the civil society, the state, international institutions, and armed groups have been powerful tools. Among them, national narratives such as epics make up a considerable part of social memory. They are used by political actors to incite adhesion to strategies, to resonate with themes and concerns which are dear to citizens. It is, thus, important to remember Jolly (2010), as he recalls the approach of Bazin (1979), in valuing the history, the political dimension, and the context of the production of epics. As epics are unearthed to serve political claims, tales of yore, trendy social and political theories, or rumors, have all been retold and weaponized by actors in conflicts.

Narratives may hold a function that allows for social and political covenants to be retold and upheld. In the case of the modern state of Mali, one must observe ancient historical recollections of colonial strife, the narrative of how Mali acquired independence from France, and more recent attempts at molding a common national Malian identity. For the purpose of this work, we will broadly examine national narratives of Mali, and most specifically those that pertain to Fula people and the political and community groups and identities that they have had to deal with in contests of violent conflict since 2012.

Mali is a very diverse country with hundreds of internal "countries," historical regions, and communities. Mali is usually presented as an heir of the Old Mali Empire that existed in West Africa between the thirteenth and the fifteenth centuries.[4] Upon acceding to independence from France in 1960, the colonies of French Sudan and Senegal decided to form the federation of Mali and break the borders designed by their soon-to-be former colonial conqueror. The initial plan for African federalism was much more grandiose. It comprised most states of what was then known as Western French Africa[5] (AOF). French Sudan and Senegal finally separated due to political tensions and rivalries between their leaders. French Sudan kept the name Mali and became an independent country on September 22, 1960. From a few million denizens in 1960, Mali is now home to some eighteen million people[6] whose native languages belong to two macro-families: Afro-Asiatic languages and Niger-Congo languages. Malians come in contrasting physical types, skin colors, and professions. Social memory is a source of data that we could not do without in the scope of this work. It is the set of historical information communities convey internally to future generations, through tales, references, remembrances, complaints, praise. Jolly (2010) points out the way in which traditional narratives are built according to specific philosophies of how power should be, as well as the identity of those enunciating them.[7] It is methodologically necessary for us to assert that our work here is not a work of philology. We are interested in classical narratives as they carry over possibilities of political appropriation by societies. They resonate with cultural contexts they appear in. Thus, they participate in the incitation of political realignment. In conflicts in Mali, just as family traditions, mass media, and fake news have been at play, so have traditional narratives. As such, they offer possibilities to investigate fuels for tensions and roads to alleviating said tensions. After all, the "Mande narrative," for instance, which we will be closely examining, has served a purpose of unity and peacebuilding in various instances. We have wished to observe the limitations of the uses of that narrative and the people's appropriation of it in recent current contexts of violence in Mali.

This work is based on an eclectic set of field data we have been collecting over the years, since the onset of the current crisis in Mali which ultimately required international support of the country in 2013. For the purpose of the argumentation we are presenting herein, we have also considered information and analyses from scientific sources, with a choice place for those works with some distance from this field and this time, so as to be able to complement factual information with in-depth musings that can shed light on political processes at hand and their implications on regional peace and security.

The data we have collected over six years was acquired thanks in large part to our involvement in human rights[8] activism in the Sahel, our numerous relationships within Fula organizations, research centers, national institutions of Mali. We have also positioned ourselves as a generally candid observer and scholar of the region, maintaining constant vigilance about events unfolding, out of personal connection with the subject at hand.[9] Throughout the hard times that have been rocking Mali, there was no question of us getting involved in conflict-solving to some extent. It simply happened. As a younger researcher, in 2012, we did not know how to get involved directly outside of an organization. What we were able to do then, and which we continued to do, was documenting acts of violence and intimidation, be it by saving files, taking screenshots of egregious incidents, or maintaining a correspondence with stakeholders, as it will become apparent in this pithy study.

We have tried to reasonably let go of any pretense of exhaustively about violent events after 2018, the initial scope of the study. Our experience in reporting human rights abuses and dealing with organizations that have been doing so for much longer[10] has proven that substance lies within qualitative accounts rather than figures that sadly become hazy and meaningless as events unfold day after day with no clear trend showing that tragedies are being curtailed. Additionally, too much information goes unreported because of the impossibility to verify it since witnesses and victims are often afraid to come forward,[11] or reaching them is a hardship of its own and those who would relay their voices would concentrate their means and powers elsewise. Unreliable sources cannot be discounted though, and this is perhaps one of the major points of interest in this work. Narratives abound, and agendas about the use of figures are rife with bias and prejudice. Until figures fully enable quick responses and actionability to protect from violence in Mali, we fear any figure will not be appropriately useful; however, much struggles of civilians are lamented over. This puts in question the very deployment of massive military operations in Mali, such as those by the MINUSMA that are often believed to endanger civilians without being able to actually predict and curtail violence. In the meantime, it is our belief that case-to-case analyses of phenomena at hand and why it is they are unfolding should be one of the pillars of research on peace in Mali. Too often, fallacious readings of the "crisis" are offered and digested as sacrosanct gospel. This affects decisions and policymaking in Mali in dramatic ways, such as when, every other week, civilians are killed because of beliefs that they had been harboring hidden sympathy for enemies of the state[12] or that they themselves were "terrorists." How did they become the enemy? Who are terrorists? Who are *the* terrorists we are enacting warfare and offensive policy over? On what grounds? What is radicalization? And how do we define vulnerability to it? Narratives used by political institutions aim to answer all these questions. Ideally.

Here, we posit that narratives that are integrated into policymaking, rules of engagement, and violence in general, stem from historical and cultural factors that are very little explained. Thus, key players of violence may make tensions and conflict worse with the bias they employ. That bias carries unsolvable damage and creates vulnerability to conversion to all forms of radicalization (ethnic and nationalistic, namely, in addition to religious radicalization).

We are focusing here on Fula as a heterogeneous community that is self-aware of its existence as a mental object for all actors of violent conflict in Mali. Indeed, even in their diversity, Fula may have been courted, feared, puzzling, seductive, for all stakeholders.

It is not the anthropology of "Fulaness" we wish to discuss here. Rather, we study mental and social projections on Fula, uses of a perceived common

Fula identity for strategic planning. These elements have drawn much interest for those who would devise field policy for peace and defense.[13] Fula have warranted several publications in the recent years, by many experts who rarely use nuance that is necessary to understand that there is not a single "Fula question" but multiple ones, from various lands and communities. This work very much dwells within the realm of mental constructions, fantasy, stereotypes, and more or less candid storytelling. All these subjective elements greatly contribute to discourses on Fula.

Fula come in many variations, and one would be hard-pressed to precisely define what makes one a Fula, other than classical sociological definitions such as patrilineal descent and self-identification. In Mali, their numbers range anywhere between three and five million individuals. There are no clear figures on how numerous they are, since the Fula ensemble is broken down into various labels (Pulaar, Fulbe, Tukulor, Wasolonka, Xaasonka, etc.), and multiple labels may be claimed. Thus, it is safe to err on the side of caution and broadly mention that they represent between 15 and 20 percent of Malians. The term "Fula Archipelago" has been favored by Boutrais (1994) refers to the disjointed continuity of Fula areas of settlement that gives Fula people a historical and geographic presence redolent of the shape of an archipelago, with islands spread over vast distances. Such is the nonexistent Fula homeland.

Fula are thought of as nomadic pastoralists because their ancestors were. Nowadays, they still retain a philosophical closeness to cow-herding and pride in cattle-ownership, but they are highly heterogeneous in their activities. This is even more true in urban settings where modes of production are dependent on the scarcity of traditional resources and a preeminence of third sector activities: traditional activities such as religious affairs, or more modern commonplace ones.

Our choice of Fula is both born of personal interests and motivated by intellectual curiosity. As a Malian of predominantly Fula ancestry, we do feel concern whenever we read the word "Fula" in any article. General news articles about victims are painful enough, but articles that position themselves as enlightened analyses of why it is "Fula" are doing whatever it is that they are said to be doing, we feel an immediate fear for what field data will be made to say. There is always, for us, concern that whatever analysis published will generalize and not account for specific circumstances. Delta "Fula" is not the same as dryland "Fula." Cleric-"Fula" are not embroidered in the same issues as camel-riding "Fula." Cosmopolitan "Fula" in the diaspora do not voice dissatisfaction toward national armies for the same reasons as Fula traveling for transhumance.[14]

Fula have had a history that is intermingled with Islamic conquest in West Africa. From the seventeenth century onward, Islamic Fula polities have ruled lands and waged war in the name of their one God. This has contributed to the shaping of stereotypes about Fula as Islamic zealots. Nevertheless, Fula herders were not always associated with these feats. Indeed, Fula societies have retained all previous modes of production, even as Islam advanced. Theocratic elites are still a minority. That has not stopped conflations between popular Fula Islam and fundamentalist armed Islam. The invasion of northern Mali by Islamic insurgents in 2012 resulted in a redistribution of power from the region of Mopti in the center of Mali to the border with Niger, eastward. Under Islamist domination, many a Fula local chief was forced into exile for fear of being victimized by the new rulers. Those Fula who remained were subjected to the same treatment as other communities. However, it should be noted that previous violent occupants, Tamasheq rebels of the MNLA[15] were largely unpopular due to looting, humiliation, and numerous acts of violence against civilians. This created a climate of discontent, adding up to the realization that local traditional elites were not able to help. Hence, when the MUJWA[16] appeared, it came in as a temporary savior and it was able to gain support from locals.

Even as the war ended and Jihadists were pushed back, the idea that some Fula had sold out lingered. The appearance of the FLM[17] in early 2015 sharpened that sentiment. Here was a new Islamist group, with a clearly professed aim of toppling state authority in Mali and establishing an Islamic state in those areas where Fula lived. They positioned themselves as scions of the former Islamic kingdom of Macina, which was ruled by Fula with an ethnocentric character. Despite harsh denouncement by descendants of the old kings of Macina, the narrative of the rebirth of Fula jihadism took fire. Even as mausoleums of the old kings were targeted by the FLM—to the horror of local Fula societies—the idea of Fula-bred terror spread out, reinforced by local micro-conflicts involving Fula and their farmer neighbors, mostly over access to pasture and lands, and also by anxious echoes of violent conflicts elsewhere in Africa where Fula were involved for myriad reasons, such as in Nigeria.[18]

The core of the present reflection lies herein. How do discourses and social memory surrounding Fula as an ensemble contribute to engagements with them, be they for partnership or for antagonism, whether by local state and international state parties or by non-state armed groups or civil society entities?

Given the tremendous amount of data about incidents in which Fula group identity is a factor at play, we will be looking at those elements that have been creating a climate for the appropriation of narratives by Fula and non-Fula, and the ways in which these are affecting conflicts in Mali. It will prove quite useful to summon information from the history of Mali and its surrounding regions, as well as an analysis of factors related to the times we live in and how they facilitate the spreading of ideas and narratives.

Thus, to make our analysis clear, we will present key elements to understanding our mixed approach to explain our analyses. Secondly, we will review Malian history and social memory. Thirdly, we will offer a commentary on the crises that have affected Mali from 2012 to 2018 and the ways in which they have affected paradigms about social life and coexistence in Mali. Lastly, it is pivotal to this work that we describe and explain narratives that specifically pertain to Fula people, both those from within their communities and those from without. Interactions between these two variables make for brokering of peace or conflict between all actors involved (states, civilians, insurgents, militias, diplomats, experts, etc.).

Fears, assumptions, and desires for reflection and teaching are the core reasons behind the inception of this work. As stories are being told and as they are shaping identity-related policies, tropes and standardized narratives nourish them for better or for worse. In analyzing types of narratives and the consequences they have had on peace and security, we will herein endeavor to provide understanding that may be useful for actors of conflicts, observers, and curious minds.

With these elements treated, we hope to be able to provide a satisfactory explanation for the topic at hand.

NOTES

1. Chapter VII specifies the terms in which the Responsibility to Protect (R2P) may be enacted. Chapter VII: Action with Respect to Threats to the Peace, Breaches of the Peace, and Acts of Aggression (1945). Retrieved from https://www.un.org/en/sections/un-charter/chapter-vii/index.html.

2. As many as 200 people have been reported as dead by locals. The attack was allegedly perpetrated by Dogon militias. On June 10, 2019, Sobaneda, a Dogon village, was attacked in what has been described as payback from Fula militias. On February 14, 2020, Ogossagou was once again attacked, as investigation reports about the 2019 massacres were being released. See: Rep. *How Much More Blood Must Be Spilled?* Human Rights Watch, February 10, 2020. https://www.hrw.org/report/2020/02/11/how-much-more-blood-must-be-spilled/atrocities-against-civilians-central-mali.

3. White, B. (August 2, 2017). Divisive Identities Cause Conflict. Retrieved from https://oicd.net/divisive-identities-cause-conflict/.

4. Ba Konaré, Konare, 198.

5. Afrique Occidentale Française.

6. Mali's population has been steadily increasing since the country became independent in 1960. World Population Dashboard Mali (2020). Retrieved from https://www.unfpa.org/data/world-population/ML.

7. "Chaque version d'un récit se construit autour d'une 'philosophie' du pouvoir qui est liée non seulement à l'identité de l'énonciateur, mais aussi aux rapports

de subordination, d'antagonisme ou de solidarité qui se manifestent au moment de l'énonciation. Toute étude sur la geste de Sunjata et sur ses variantes exige donc de rapporter ces textes, d'une part, à leurs modalités d'énonciation cérémonielle, et, d'autre part, à la situation sociale et politique de ceux qui ont pour fonction de les énoncer, en considérant aussi bien le passé que le présent."

8. We have been the leader of Kisal. We founded this organization in 2013 at the behest of Fula community leaders looking to advocate for the rights of herders in the Sahel. In this work, we are not basing our data and analysis specifically on Kisal material. That is a task we have undertaken elsewhere.

9. Though of transnational ancestry that is mostly Fula, all four of our grandparents were born in present-day Mali. We have spent all our childhood and adolescence, as well as various episodes of adulthood in Mali. It is our home country.

10. Such as Human Rights Watch.

11. This is not an absolute truth, as Kisal's experience has been proving for years. When speaking with trusted community-adjacent people, witnesses and victims have shown a staunch desire to be heard. And even with little attention, they can seize a momentum and voice their sufferings and concerns. Even these littlest of concerns are too often missing from the fields they are in, be they remote areas, or even urban centers.

12. During interview in Bamako on June 8, 2018, with an officer of the Malian army, we were able to get access to an internal source explaining how recruits far from their homes often viewed any Fula in the bush as a potential terrorist. This sometimes had unfortunate consequences such the subsequent Boulikessi 2018 incident in which a terrified soldier killed some twelve civilians. See: Rfi. (June 26, 2018). La Minusma confirme une bavure de militaires maliens du G5 Sahel à Boulikessi. Retrieved July 4, 2020, from http://www.rfi.fr/fr/afrique/20180627-minusma-bavure-militaires-maliens-g5-sahel-boulikessi.

13. We have participated in several closed seminars with officials of various countries in order to explain the "Fula question," starting from 2015.

14. Transhumance is a short-term annual migratory journey. Fula identity is closely linked to cattle-herding. Fula herders are practitioners of transhumance. They go on transhumance in order to find pasture for their cattle, to alleviate pressure from green areas already grazed on, and more generally to sustain their lifestyle as herders. Transhumance is dotted with rites and traditions, many of which serve to prepare youths for their duties as adults, and taking over herds. Though families go on transhumance together, not all members go. Communities always have a "homeland," that is, a dwelling, a village, a city, or an encampment which they view as theirs and where they settle down at the beginning of the rainy season, around the month of May. This is when they have their homecoming, as nature becomes bountiful. At the onset of the dry season, around October, herds and folks renew their travels.

15. Mouvement National de Libération de l'Azawad: National Movement for the Liberation of Azawad.

16. The Movement for Unity and Jihad in West Africa. It was an offshoot of Al-Qaeda in the Islamic Maghreb (AQIM), with an intent to create indigenous hotspots for jihadism.

17. Front de Libération du Macina: Front for the Liberation of Macina. An islamist group promoting Jihadist hegemony. They took up the name of the historical Jihadist Fula kingdom of Macina.

18. Herdsmen killings: Buhari dey sleep on top bicycle. Wole Soyinka (February 13, 2018). Retrieved July 5, 2020, from https://www.bbc.com/pidgin/tori-43041267.

Chapter 1

Theoretical Framing of Narratives and Stereotypes

COMBINING FIELDS OF STUDY

As we extract data from anthropological, historical, and political sources, we endeavor to remain careful and observe resonance with our own person and clinical experiences to avoid expected bias. In noting this, we hereby formally acknowledge that this work stems in major part from ecological self-observation among Fula individuals and associations, in Mali and in the global Fula diaspora around the world.

This section, meant to dissect our theoretical approach to this work, aims to—hopefully—make clearer how we have gone about observing and analyzing data. "Clinical" means "at the bedside." Indeed, it is in proximity to urban centers that we have enriched our data. Humility and clarification of our position are inherent to how we have been working. Hence this work will surely be different from that of other authors coming from different backgrounds, with more systematic data completion. We considered those paths to be valid. Ours is what it is. With it, we would like it to explore and understand how distant and seemingly smaller events create massive effects the public yearns to understand. These events are often presented without subtext that may help in acting with better ethics and consideration for the needs of those people, those Fula, who have been ambivalent sources of interest.

International relations and political science are core components of analysis of a transnational people such as Fula and their stories as victims or actors with agency in a context of prolonged tensions. Complementing them, our initial background as a clinical psychologist[1] has been crucial in making sense of individual or group understandings and actions based on identity narratives. This has been helping to shape our vision of political and social events over the years. We have written several times[2] about these specific types of combinations of discipline from our particular perspective.[3] Researching transgenerational[4] fluxes in Fula identity, we have had to delve into anthropology from a clinical psychology perspective. This approach is similar to that of Riesman (1998) who spent time among the Jelgooji Fula in northern Burkina Faso. Immersed among the local Fula, he had intimate access to life stories, remembrance of times past, and narratives about migrations and identity. Riesman explained how this data impacted him on a personal level. He became able to better understand how individual stories combined with group narratives were a core element of how this community differentiates itself from outside communities.

Similarly, through observation of lore and tradition and discourses about oneself and present communities, we have constituted a corpus of knowledge that helps to understand how emotions and attachment to self and identity mold present strife and conflicts.

Unearthing multiple sources and interviewing in close, clinical processes may yield ordinary and intimate stories that help make sense of historical positions and current stances and claims based on seemingly vague or unrelated reasons. These claims and stances may have deeper roots than they appear to at first. In this work, several examples of how apparently innocuous stories carry over violence will be showcased.

We will delve into the politics of war and community identity in Mali. With our dual background and prior study of Fula, we have been able to propose recognized interpretations of stories from the fields that we have observed from interviews over ten year, studying Fula lives and trajectories.[5] Anthropology has been useful for understanding underlying concepts and organizations of Fula social life and expression of identity.[6] History has been allowing us to further connect present trends with past occurrences and to better analyze current Fula narratives and how they may connect with past trajectories now updated.[7] Political science allows us to describe events in the making. It permits live comparisons between our experience and contemporary original data and points of view offered by fellow academics and experts such as Cissé (2018). His and other native political scientists have thoroughly explained how armed groups vie for hegemony in majority Fula territories. Back and forth and cross-study between sources enable a holistic vision of identity-building and how it is used either to promote a community or to harm it.

CONSTRUCTING NARRATIVES, GROUP IDENTITIES, AND STEREOTYPES

A 2017 OICD paper by Bruce Shaw indicates that culture and identity are featured in some 60 percent of all human conflicts. It is nigh impossible to dissociate identity and political discourse. Identity is an essential component of conflict emergence. Fula-Dogon clashes that became visible as soon as spring 2012 should be proof enough that economy, development, or political rivalries alone cannot explain deteriorating relationships between neighbors. Governance is a necessity for maintaining peace between communities with deep antagonisms. In 2012 Mali, as soon as state governance disappeared, violence erupted. What happened, then? All factors must be looked up. Simplifying intercommunal tensions as temporary rifts between neighbors does disservice to all parties.

It is precisely with such ideas that we approach Fula identity tensions in Mali, wondering how they have become a source of both fascination and oversimplification in order to placate governments and give hope about a future that could be peaceful with investments in development.

One factor that may negatively cause friction between Fula and their neighbors is depictions of Fula as fundamental Islamists. These rely on the social memory of jihads led by Fula clerics, most notably in the nineteenth century.[8] As modern-day Fula deny the wrongdoings of their ancestors' jihads on their neighbors, and as official Malian history glamorizes past kingdoms as great achievements of Mali, symbolic pain and individual trauma in communities impacted is eschewed. Rage from state-directed unity narratives brushing off these pain and trauma, contributing to identities of revolt. In a self-fulfilling prophecy, it should not be surprising that Fula laypersons themselves would embrace rebellion as defense against narrative-fueled aggressions by their neighbors, confirming bias against them. All parties keep being considered as objects to be studied and essentialized, in order to better categorize them in peacemaking and development strategies.

Our meetings in the field raised a topic that seems central to us: the place that groups can occupy in the investments they make in their fights. That is one instance in which we must summon our reflections based on psychology. Kaes (2000) offers a theory explaining the use by groups of what he calls "the group psychic device," a device such as a "psychic envelope signifying the demarcation" of the group with another group. Members of a group build together a system of relationships and operations that maintain feelings of continuity of existence and reduce group anxiety. They create group myths or narratives that they may positively identify with. The construction of a group psychic device offers mediation between inner emotions and external hardships. This also makes it possible to account for groupthink. Myths, narratives, and ambitions combine with intents, and help mold reality (Eliade, 2016). These phenomena contribute to needs for protection of one's group, need for borders, positive distinction from other. Groups may extend their membership and characteristics in order to acquire more strength against aggression. This mechanism will be observable in the stories in this work. Kinship and loyalty allow for reaffirmation of the feeling of belonging together. Narratives are variables operating in these processes. As such, they may integrate necessary differentiation and antagonisms with groups deemed as potentially dangerous. Herein lie bases for the creation and use of stereotypes. Unfortunate stereotypes about all communities have endangered visions of neighbors. Stereotypes are mechanisms that simplify mental processes.[9] They allow cognitive economy-saving, even-more-so in contexts of high violence. With deep-seated narratives of antagonism, stereotypes are mobilized to recruit emotional "allyship" both for the in-group and for the out-group. In doing so, the combination of preexisting narratives with stereotypes may create self-fulfilling prophecies rationalizing any action by purported antagonists.

Fula group identity discourses are built on perceptions of who is Fula and what makes it possible to distinguish Fula from others. Extensive literature exists on the different social categories of the "Fula Archipelago."[10] There exists a strong sense of in-group versus out-group in representations of Fula and narratives around them. It should not be denied that identity is integral part of society dynamics and intergroup and internal relationships, such as conflicts. Hence, it is important to solidify group narratives. And this is how narratives are needed as one essential tool. This is why narratives must be thought of in analyses of group relationships.

ETHNICITY AS A DEVICE FOR UNITY

Mali is to be understood not as one country that has emerged upon colonization but as a land of confluences. Even in saying this very obvious fact, we are already stating a narrative that is summoned time and again by proponents of the "Pax Mali narrative,"[11] to justify the need for peace talks, integration, unicity, and so on. Looking at Mali, this sizeable territory in the middle of northwestern Africa, one cannot help but notice the incredible diversity of the land: the Sahara, the semi-arid Sahel, savannah, and bushes.

"Ethnic group" has been used by Western anthropologists to refer to the various common lineage and language communities living in non-European territories at the time of the colonial enterprise (Amselle, M'Bokolo, 1999). By this term are designated human groups considered homogeneous, sharing common cultural elements, language, and origins. Ethnicity is above all a common descent in the context of the Mali and its neighboring sub-Saharan African countries (Keïta, 2009). Thus, ethnicity is mainly based on the awareness of having a common past made up of blood alliances, usually through paternal lines in most societies of Mali. But, in addition to shared ancestry or language, cultural elements such as mythology and shared rites unite groups of people as an ethnic group. Fula have fascinated colonizers from the times when they first met them in Africa (Monteil, 1950). The "red people" also described by Pondopoulo, referring to Fula and their neighbors, became an object of fascination by colonizers who were intent on distinguishing them as a group separate from other peoples of western Africa. Still, prior to the arrival of colonizers, as Pondopoulo explains, Fula possessed a deep sense of who they were, irrespective of outside discourses. Hence, Fula, though a disparate people, should be considered a group that recognizes itself as a homogenous entity when it comes to claiming social struggle and defend common identity on extra-Fula stages. As previously explained, groups function as devices meant to protect device that protect. In reflections we shared in 2013, we stated how Fula found internal and emotional power in remembrance of their differences from their neighbors. We observed Fula from various countries and observed how they claimed a common way of functioning as well as commonly shared physicality. These claims went beyond socially, anthropologically, and physically perceptible differences. In our field experience, several instances of this phenomenon were visible. For instance, search of some keywords on social media yielded disparate results showcasing only images of what was considered to be Fula-adjacent, and what was fantasied to be related to Fula identity. Objective reality did not matter so much as appropriation of narratives and emotions in order to create new connections, extending borders of "Fulaness." Pictures of Ethiopians and other non-Fula Sudanese are used by some Fula. Hashtags such as #LenyolGootol ("One people, one language") are meant to be banners unifying Fula. Yet, not all Fula speak Fula languages, and not all people claiming Fulaness identify as only Fula. Even illness may be appropriated to participate in "The Fula Experience"[12] (Gordon, 2000). This goes on to show how identity and narratives are employed to find support and unity that is needed in times of duress, joining faraway peoples within one same cause. Pride appears as a function of defense. Psychological processes of shortening distances stem from shared narratives about what oneself should be, regardless of situations. Narratives and pride are tapped into in order to garner unity or to rally to common causes. In our experiences with Fula organizations, we have been able to witness this in real settings where Fula from multiple countries would join in festivals, WhatsApp group chats, or radio shows.[13] Narration and pride are sentiments that contributed in fostering transnational movements that would later on use these sentiments of unity to summon help in contexts of violent action. This goes on to show some articulation between narrative-built unity and actions in the field. For instance, in January 2017, while in Mali, we received a call from a distraught Mauritanian Fula living in France, lamenting over Fula massacres happening in Mali, and calling for protests by Fula from the diaspora. This goes on to show how global

Fula unity manifests itself exponentially in our current era of the advent of new technologies of information. Psychological mechanisms should not be discounted when observing and analyzing trends in violent conflicts. Fula's narratives on themselves cannot be discounted from the understanding of inter-Fula allyship and internal dissensions. Divergences exist in in-groups, usually in more specific and low-level tensions. At higher and more visible levels, common identity is meant to placate or to enlist in common endeavors. This may make it possible to either mediate or silence grievances. It blurs lines between different Fula communities. They become somewhat implicated in matters of other Fula groups. This leads to conflating all Fula together and making all of them fall under the same stereotypes. Hence, nuance and ambivalence are indispensable components of Fula identity, meaning it is impossible to mention Fula issues without deep understanding of in-group dynamics and how they are projected on the outside, even more so in times of duress.

NOTES

1. We graduated from Université Paris Descartes (France) in 2013, with a psychology doctorate thesis on "The Functions of Religion in Mali: Study on a Malian Muslim Population."
2. This article was written at a time when there was still a systematic refusal by the Malian government to admit that violence in central Mali may have roots in intercommunal tensions. https://theconversation.com/central-mali-gripped-by-a-dangerous-brew-of-jihad-revolt-and-self-defence-67668.
3. Ba Konare, D. A. (2018, September 4). En Afrique, le fantasme d'une "communauté peule " radicalisée. Retrieved from https://theconversation.com/en-afrique-le-fantasme-dune-communaute-peule-radicalisee-102276.
4. Konaré, 2011.
5. Konaré, 2010, 2013, 2018, 2019.
6. Dupire, 1970.
7. Pondopoulo, 2009.
8. Robinson, 1985.
9. Ka, 2013.
10. Notably Dupire (1970), and Kyburtz (1994).
11. In this political narrative that is often summoned, Mali is purported to be a country of peaceful peoples living in a melting pot under one government. Such is the inarguable nature of the "Mali Peace."
12. In a study on Fula of the Guinean Highlands, A.J. Gordon noted how complaints about illness reasserted how Fula originated from other lands and thus were different from native peoples they conquered and mostly replaced. By speaking about their physiques as alien, they somewhat set boundaries to what the Fula experience was, all the while uniting under common sufferings and narratives of migration. The

reality of "population replacement" is not so simple, however, and may be studied elsewhere.

13. We ourselves were invited to speak at Fula rallies in the United States in July 2013, August 2013, January 2014, and July 2017. We are nowhere near fluent in any Fula language. At least some fifteen countries are represented in major international "Pan-Fula" gatherings. Every time, unity is the benevolent discourse and wish, with narratives of perpetual Fula sufferings and needs for solidarity, as well as a renewal of a covenant to be one people.

Chapter 2

Narrating Mali and Malians

COMMUNITIES AND CASTES

With the independence and the emergence of modern states in Africa, ethnic groups and formerly peoples have become closer to each other. Additionally, urbanization and state cultural policies have given prominence to certain languages and cultures over others. Groups formerly living far apart are now brought together by nation-building. They experience intermingling within a fledgling nation seeking unity. Urban areas highlight the development of a new culture, a somewhat mixed culture. Elements from different culture are sheered away, in compromise. This is the case in Bamako, Segou, or Mopti, hotspots of political activity. In this work, we prefer the use of the term "community," and we favor a vision of groups of people based first and foremost on expressions of belonging together within an ensemble. That idea means that an individual may identify as a Fula, and a Dogon, at the same time, though anthropologically these identities could cancel each other out if the rule of patrilineal descent is applied as a strict criterion for group acceptance.[1] Throughout history, though, this rule has not been applied *stricto sensu*, as the case of the Songhay Arma[2] demonstrates, among other cases. Community mixing, formerly commonplace in certain regions, is much more frequent nowadays. Thus, the boundaries of belonging to one ethnic group or another become blurred over time, even though ethnic awareness remains omnipresent.[3] As the role of traditional initiation has diminished as a result of changing livelihoods, urban identity takes over and individuals are made less familiar with their identity. This is not a systematic and strict situation, however. Ethnic awareness is still very present, and it is still visible through family name, community, and hometown[4] for everyone. Upon first meeting a person, their name and their hometown help in socializing with them.

Depending on these, references and acceptable codes and behaviors become known. From there power dynamics may become visible, as well. However, application of these elements is obviously subject to individual contexts and social and political backgrounds. In a typical meeting, you would greet each other, ask names, and sometimes hometown. These elements give indications on the lineage, community, and social position of the interlocutor.

In this work, we will mainly be focusing on four peoples, in addition to Fula[5] people: *Maninka*[6], *Bambanan*[7], *Tamasheq*[8], and *Dogon*.

The Mande-Bamanan ensemble is an old people that is a surviving remnant of the ancient Mali Empire.[9] Their language family, the Mande languages, is the most widely spoken one in Mali. They constitute the first community in Mali in terms of population number.

Tamasheq peoples are of high interest because they have launched various rebellions in Mali since the country's independence in 1960. These rebellions have had lasting impacts every time they occurred: in the early 1960s, in the early 1990s, in the mid-2000s, and in 2011.[10] They have left the country weaker, all the while opening discussions about inclusivity and the place of faraway marginalized communities in the social and political fabric of Mali.

Fula communities are the single most numerous people in sub-Saharan Africa, though no conclusive data exists about their precise numbers. In Mali, they represent the second community ensemble. They are made up of various subgroups, not all of which speak the same language but acknowledge kinship with each other. Their numbers and their strong attachment to a common identity have made them a subject of interest in times when Mali has been vying for ways of reshaping its multiple identities. Fula inhabit almost all regions of Mali. They are also present in all government institutions. Their history of hegemony and jihad has brought concerns about their identity and how it is shaking up a Malian national identity.

Dogon are the least numerous of the peoples we will be mentioning in this work. They are no lesser, though. Dogon have created fascination with colonizers and foreigners in general for decades. They were ruled by Fula overlords during the times of the Macina jihad, in the early nineteenth century.[11] Since the independence in 1960, they have been attracting great interest because of their culture, the charm of their habitat, high tourism potential in the "Dogon Country."[12] They also possess a strong educated diaspora throughout Mali. Currently, Dogon identity is reasserting itself in a bold manner, at a time when jihadist threat is reawakening past wounds as it echoes submissions past. Contrarily to news media sensalization of Fula-Dogon conflicts into the classic trope and narratives of Muslims versus Christians or Pagans, Dogon are by far a more Muslim than they are Christian of Pagan. However, it must be noted that no conclusive data can be cited to further this point. We must rely on personal experience and testimonies of Dogon individuals we have met in Mali.

In addition to cultural and lineage communities, most Malian societies are broken down into castes. Castes represent a system that still exists throughout Mali, though their status is not present in the Malian constitution. Slavery used to be a component of this system. The number of castes may vary according to the society being examined. Most societies typically exhibit three main categories that are classified along a descending hierarchy: free folks and the nobility; masters of arts and crafts; and, finally, hereditary captives and slaves.

During colonization, the existence of local slavery was employed as an argument to further subjugate natives, deeming them barbarian and non-egalitarian unlike Western societies. Since slavery had recently been outlawed in all French territories, imperial French rulers decided that their mission of civilizing Africans meant taking responsibility for correcting the ills of their societies.[13] In all likelihood, this narrative of "civilizing" certainly brought more fuel to the case for imperial conquest of bountiful lands and investment into the colonial machine. These same arguments were used elsewhere to subjugate natives, heathens, barbarians, such as in the Americas.

Societies of Mali, with their many layers and components, each possess narratives about their origins and rationalizations of inequalities within them or their attitudes toward other communities. For instance, to better understand tensions and claims between peoples in central Mali, it is important to know what each community thinks of the other and how their social memories narrate their own history with regards to their rivals and neighbors. The case of opposing narratives of wars past between Dogon and Fula accurately illustrates this point.

PRAISING SELF-NARRATION

In Mali, the griot tradition has been a powerful source for social memory, in addition to more informal oral traditions. The caste of griots are bards, hereditary masters of tongue and song, historians. They are deemed to be "praise-singers" as their vast knowledge and art are not only limited to narration but also to eulogy.[14] The art of bards in telling proper stories to their audiences is a valued practice throughout societies of Mali, and the Western Sudan in general. Griot tradition is present in all these societies in one form or the other. Griots are in charge of aggrandizing clans, lionizing individuals, and consecrating narratives. Their functions are not questioned. This has brought on the existence of parallel narratives pertaining to one same topic or space. Griots are acknowledged as custodians of oral tradition, with all the caveats that may require. Their tales are concomitantly held along those of written sources such as the Arabic language sources that are the Tarikh al Sudan, and the Tarikh al Fattash, colonial writings, and academic publications. Indeed, multiple handles exist, to better understand societies of the Western Sudan.

Griots are an inestimable source of information, be they from the Malian regions of Adrar, Macina, Birgo, or Wassolou, and so on. Their social functions are many and omnipresent. They are stewards of social ceremonies (naming, weddings, funerals, coming-of-age rites, etc.), confidantes to leaders, summoners of tradition, wise folks, knowers of things occult. Indeed, in the Maninka[15] language, they are one of the *Nyamakala*,[16] along with smiths (Keita, 2010). "Nyamakala" is made up of the word *nyama*[17] and *kala*.[18] While smiths destroy material threats with fire and arms, griots defuse immaterial threats with words and songs. Praising and recalling glory are powerful tools to ensconce power, prestige, and durability. This is made visible in social gatherings when griots repeat several times patronyms, clan names, ceremonial titles, great deeds, lineages, and so on. Each griot line is intertwined with the line of a single prestigious household and people whose history they must learn and pass on to their descendants. To illustrate this point, we may give the example of our paternal line. Our patronym is Konaare, our clan name is Mansare. Our ancient origin is Mande, though our ancestors have established many roots during sojourns in the historical regions of Kala, Karta, and Xaaso. Our "hometown" is Segala, which we have never been to. During ceremonies, all these elements are recalled, with minute precision, to assert the validity of our nobility and our claims to whatever endeavor being executed. Every single one of these elements is important and remains strongly associated with both group and personal narratives. A patronym is thus not just a name, but indeed a "good name." Its knowledge alone orientates toward the way to treat individuals and groups. It is only natural, then, that Fula literally refers to these patrilineal family names as "praise-names" (*Yettoode*). The existence of griots means that narratives are precious and that they are meticulously passed down in societies of Mali, with all the subjectivity and aggrandizement they hold. Griotic traditions contribute to strengthening group devices and reinforcing pride and power in inner narratives. In ancient times, griots would praise warriors before battles to imbue into them spiritual strength. Nowadays, griots continue their tasks in more restrained circumstances, but they readily contribute to popularization of narratives, oftentimes after paid orders from public figures and political personalities. Their using popular music has also kept them relevant to this day, with the glamour and passion associated with pop stars.

Beyond the current functions griots occupy, they are great embodiments of Malian societies in search of memory, pride, and self-sustaining narratives which may become dangerous when they preclude facing real stories in the making and when they contribute in reinforcing narratives that hide away estimations of weaknesses.

QUESTIONING THE *PAX MALI*?

Mali was named Sudan during the times of French colonization. It is part of a historical region known since ancient times as "the Sudan." The Sudan is the name of the regions that are south of the Sahara Desert and which represent a contact zone between northern Africa and the rest of the continent. The "*Bilad as-Sudan*" means the country of the Blacks. This location name encompasses all lands inhabited by darker-skinned Africans, generally. The term "Sudan" has come to refer to three countries: French Sudan (modern-day Mali), South Sudan, and Sudan. The Sudan encompasses the Sahel.[19] In historical terms, the Western Sudan refers to realms between the Atlantic and the Adrar-n-Ifoghas, from west to east, and between the Sahara and the savannah, from north to south. This area is centered around the Republic of Mali.

In present-day Malian political administration, below the central level, there exist regions divided into "cercles" (literally, "circles"). Each cercle is made up of several communes among which six constitute the special territory of the capital city, the "District of Bamako." Each cercle is comprised of a chef-lieu de cercle (the cercle capital). The lowest administrative territories are communes, which are sometimes made up of several settlements and types of settlements (towns, villages, encampments, etc.).

Malian regimes at the times of the crisis whose beginnings are officially set to 2012 had been relying on rule by consensus, with little opposition and with a plebiscite of presidential decisions. During the rule of an ethnic Fula president, Amadou Toumani Touré, a *Pax Mali* narratives was frequently employed in political discourses and narratives about a united and harmonious Mali. To paraphrase André Bourgeot in 2013,[20] Mali's societies had been relying on "consensual democracy" and that permissively silenced problems and eluded aspirations of peoples. Henceforth, it is no surprise that the crisis in Mali appeared as such a sudden cataclysm both to people outside of conflict zones and to external observers. It had been long in the making. But before the altar of the *Pax Mali* narrative, there was no space for questioning and discussing complexities of Malian identities. We have faced this very issue in 2012, as we were writing a sardonic journalistic piece on the Mande[21] bases of Malian society. A scholar who we asked for an opinion on the draft declared: "*Why would you break open doors which we have already busted through? Identity is not an issue in Mali. We are past this, and we have resolved this. Do not stir the pot and make trouble.*" Indeed, detailing the complexities and nuances of identity-caused suffering in Mali proved to be troublesome and a danger to social peace which fellow countrymen were eager to keep. Many a time, we have heard: "*Mali is not like those forest countries of Africa*"; "*We are too civilized for war*"; "*See how these people kill each other by the dozen, this could never happen here.*" And yet, war broke out, and the peaceful Mali that was so desperately wished for ceased to exist. Yet, this narrative, these mental images, these faithful wishes linger, still. Even as further past the 2012 beginning of the Malian crisis, in 2018, on several occasions, members of the Malian government have said that there is no war in Mali, but only a problem of "residual insecurity"[22] and terrorism. Terrorism was the problem. And Mali had to wage a war on terror to bring back its legendary peacefulness.

THE MEANING OF MALI

Jolly (2010) explains how the epic of Sunjata Keyta, the founder of the Mali Empire, has been used at the time of the independence in Mali to build a sense of national identity, and to ensconce the country into a common narrative.[23] Belonging to a common narrative is a concern that is served more often than not to strengthen adhesion to a common struggle.

The Epic of Mande is one of the best-known historical narratives of Africa. It is at once an account of a then-unprecedented political and social upheaval in the western Sudan, and a legendary tale of heroism and ambition by its leading figure, King Sunjata Keyta of Mande. Sunjata is described as a magical prince born from the marriage of King Nare Fa Makan Konate of the Mansare[24] clan of the kingdom of Mande[25] and the Buffalo Woman Sogolon Jata. After being foretold by mystical hunters that their prize for a successful hunt, Sogolon the buffalo witch-woman, would bear the greatest lord to have ever walked the earth, King Nara Fa Makan agreed to wed and (with great difficulty) bed the lady as his second wife. Sogolon Keju (Sogolon the Ugly) would, in time, give birth to Sunjata after an incredibly long mythical pregnancy. The legend tells that Sunjata could not walk until age seven, when, after continuous teasing by the entourage of the first royal wife, Sasuma of the Berete noble ancient family, Sunjata took courage, crawled to an esteemed smith of the realm, and asked of him to forge the heaviest and most impressive metal crutches. To the surprise of the whole clan, Sunjata "the Lame" not only finally got up and walked with the support of the crutches, but he also proved to possess superhuman strength. He who was made fun of for not being able to climb trees and get fruit for his mother, now uprooted a whole tree and brought it to his mother. From that day forth, Sunjata no longer amused. He became a danger to the royal claim of his half-brothers. The years to come were to be dark years: the king died, Sogolon Jata and her brood were exiled to neighboring Mande folks provinces, the realm was invaded by a powerful witch-king who dabbled in the dark arts and controlled the powers of metallurgy so revered and feared. This man, Sumaworo Kante of the Soso, is remembered as the Vulture King. Upon his conquests, Sumaworo defeated Sunjata's elder brother and took his half-sister Nana Triban, a legendary beauty, for wife, connecting his blood with that of the people of Mande and asserting his claim.

The denouement of the epic is reached when Sunjata, victor over the evil Smith King Sumaworo Kante, in 1235, gathers all the lords of the realm to pledge allegiance to his power and to swear fealty to a charter remembered as the Charter of Kurukan Fuga. This Charter of Mande is considered by both Malians and Guineans as evidence of the greatness of their history. For, in a time when Europe is said to have been ravaged by violence, plague, and obscurantism, there, thrived in the heart of Africa a kingdom of gentlemen, capable of producing the "first democratic constitution of the modern era."[26]

The Epic of Mande, with its continued rediscovery during colonization and since independence, plots the history of ancient Mali as the founding episode of the greatness of modern Mali. Although great empires had existed in the area of present-day Mali before the time of Mande/Mali,[27] the idea of the Charter of Mande as an egalitarian and humanistic code of law and conduct (Keita, 2010) earned the Mali Empire prestige that no other polity before could boast. While it is most certainly true that the subsequent Songhay Empire was vaster, more powerful, and overall wealthier, Mande, at its peak, was far more revered across the world. Depictions of the lavish lifestyles of its Mansa (emperors) are told in European and Middle Eastern tomes. The journey of Mansa Kanku Musa to Mecca and back is well documented. This Malian emperor of the thirteenth century has recently been described as one of the wealthiest men to have ever lived.[28]

The Mali Empire spanned territories from present-day Gambia to Niger, and from the North of Mali to the North of Côte d'Ivoire. This specific geographical location means it encompasses almost all of modern Mali. And so, it has come to be conflated with its namesake modern republic. That conflation is at the core of nationalist rhetoric in Mali, for, in taking pride in Mali, it is the legacy of Mande that is reappropriated, and the people of Mande that are exalted. Though the Mali Empire came to be multiethnic and highly cosmopolitan for its time, boasting relationships with the Mediterranean world, the Gulf of Guinea, and as far as Asia, it is unclear how much of the imperial spirit trickled down to the little people, to minor peoples within the realm. Even as great cities Djenne or Timbuktu, outside of the Mande Heartland, took over as metropolizes of the empire, the epic of Sunjata still arguably remains the most prestigious tale of Malian glory. Other peoples of Mali than the Mandeka could claim glory from the times of the empire. However, own national narratives do not necessarily speak of self-agency during the olden days of Mali. This has the consequence of making the Republic of Mali the heir of a realm that is not representative of all the current peoples of Mali. A country as diverse and plural as Mali possesses rich lore and myriads of epics and lineages that never appear as emblems of its national identity. This fact allows for contestation of Mali's acknowledgment (or lack thereof) of all its components, and so, it paves the way for self-affirmation by groups seeking more national recognition and better symbolic representation within the republic. Arguments against Mali's legitimacy majorly rest on this idea.

Radio Rurale de Guinée, Intermédias Consultants (Switzerland), the Centre d'études Linguistiques et Historiques par la Tradition Orale (CELHTO, Niger), with the support of the Organisation de la Francophonie, organized a formal gathering in March 1998 in Guinea's Kankan, with participants from Guinea, Mali, Burkina Faso, and Senegal. Siriman Kouyaté,[29] one of the participants of the workshop, was given the task of proposing a final text reprising the Epic of Mande. That rendition was comprised of forty-four articles. This was a situation in which ancient traditions have been tapped into to formalize a code of law that countries may take pride in. In doing this, though, however grand and inspiring the deed, other communities were neglected. Law, history, and tradition were merged under the authority of the anointed designer, Siriman Kouyaté. Precepts of law, morals, customs, are thus laid down for posterity, and for employ in solving differences and bringing people from a shared geographical and cultural continuum together, though many continuums and spaces may be superimposed on each other as is wont to happen systematically in the Western Sudan.

Over the years, the text that was produced would come to be finalized after several discussions and be released as its latest form in 2008. Ever since, Mali has proposed the Charter of Kurukan Fuga as an item of international immaterial heritage, with the UNESCO.

It is to be understood that Kurukan Fuga was deemed "Partition of the world," for it truly was a feat that delineated the known peoples and vassals thereby under the sway of Mande, and the codes for proper interactions and justice. Under Mande, all peoples would have a place of their own. They could belong together within one narrative.

However consensual the Charter of Mande is meant to appear, the truth is that its origins vary greatly according to those who speak about it. Hunters from Mali, griots from Guinea and from the royal Malian Mande city of Kangaba do not agree about whether the Charter was set in front of an assembly in what would appear as a democratic way. A shard of evidence that the Charter holds hidden esotericism can be found in the septennial retellings of the Charter between noblemen of the Keyta clan of Kangaba and their griots (Jolly, 2010). No assembly is allowed. Foreigners may be invited, but only sitting outside of gathering halls, unable to hear what has been retold for tens of generations. The secrecy of the retellings asserts the solemnity of the Charter. Rather than a legislative text, it would be an aristocratic edict come top-down to the people.

It is quite interesting to consider the Charter as a multifaceted ambivalent text. This is very much in line with popular receptions of the text and its symbolism. On the one hand, Malians are called to accept democracy as a participatory process, just as their alleged ancestors did before them. It is all about inclusivity and co-building, then. But on the other hand, the good gospel of the Charter is to be accepted as a fully comprehensive text delineating the needs and moral vicissitudes of citizens. Like dogma, it is to be accepted and not questioned. Again, this ambivalence echoes the peculiar nature of Mali's democracy, between submission and defiance based on narratives.

NOTES

1. Patrilinear affiliation is the norm in the Western Sudan.
2. The Songhay Arma are descendants of Moroccan envoys that came to northern Mali as conquerors in the late sixteenth century. After Morocco defeated Songhay forces, some of the Moroccans remained in the newly created Moroccan Pashalik (province) and married native women of Songhay background. Thus, the Songhay Arma came into existence. They are acknowledged as part of Songhay communities, with dual recognition of this heritage and their Moroccan roots as well. Unlike some ethnic Arabs of Mali who also boast Moroccan paternal descent, they do not identify as Arabs or Moroccans first, though. Hence, ethnicity and sense of community are dependent on multiple factors.
3. Ndiaye, 1996.
4. In a Malian context, hometown does not refer to the place where when grew of lives in. Rather, the term indicates the settlement where their community belong and have belonged to for generations. The word varies depending on communities. In the Bambanan language, the word is *dugu*. In some Fula dialects, the word *wuro* is used. They respectively mean "land," and "village"/"settlement."
5. Fula are known as *Peul* in French. They usually call themselves Fulɓe, although this may vary depending on context and area. They are called Fulani in Nigeria and in English materials. We have chosen the term "Fula" as it is most used in Mali, but more importantly, it possesses the root "Ful" which is used in Fula languages to designate Fula individuals. A Fula is called a Pullo. The plural is Fulɓe. The "p" sound is merely a consonant mutation of the sound "f." Consonant mutations are an essential feature of Fula languages.
6. Also known as Malinke (literally: those from Mali, the ancient kingdom).
7. Also known as Bambara.
8. They usually refer to themselves as the "Kel Tamasheq," the people of the Tamasheq language.
9. The Mali Empire was prominent between the thirteenth and fifteenth centuries.

10. Lecocq & Klute, 2013.
11. Sanankoua, 1990.
12. Dogon communities live on hills, by caverns, and in dryland, near Fula herders and Bozo fisherpeople.
13. Ba Konaré & Konaré, 1983.
14. Barry, 2011.
15. Maninka or Mandeka means "from Mande." This also refers to a present-day community.
16. The middle rank in the caste hierarchy.
17. Malevolent energy, grudge.
18. Spear, rod.
19. In Arabic, Sahel means "*border*." Nowadays, it broadly refers to the semi-arid lands around the southern borders of the Sahara, from Mauritania to Sudan.
20. "A l'évidence, la démocratie consensuelle, favorise (voire institutionnalise) le ou les pouvoirs en place en le légitimant implicitement. Elle secrète une illusoire paix sociale tout en transférant les contradictions inhérentes à toute société et à tout système politique en un avenir flou et diffus qui empêche toute élaboration de stratégies politiques visant à résoudre autant que faire se peut, les problèmes auxquels chaque société est confrontée et masque les enjeux de pouvoirs qui n'ont plus la possibilité de s'exprimer publiquement. Ce type de démocratie opacifie les relations sociales et politiques tout en maintenant du lien social (au profit du pouvoir en place) d'où sa force et sa faiblesse et donc ses limites dans les phénomènes de régulation sociale de la conflictualité" (Op-Ed in Le Journal, republished on various Malian media, February 12, 2014).
21. Mande is the kingdom from which the Mali Empire was born. It is viewed as a birthrock of Malian glory, of sorts.
22. In focusing on the idea of a residual insecurity, Malian authorities seemed tone-deaf in their public discourse about popular grievances, L. (January 8, 2018). L'Indicateur du Renouveau. Retrieved July, from https://www.maliweb.net/editorial/linsecurite-residuelle-na-716-morts-mali-2017-2730288.html.
23. "Énoncée généralement par des griots mandingues, l'épopée de Sunjata raconte l'histoire du fondateur de l'empire médiéval du Mali. Dès la création de la République du Mali en 1960, ce récit est fréquemment mobilisé pour construire une identité nationale et pour légitimer les choix politiques du nouvel État. Près de quarante ans plus tard, l'une des conséquences de ce processus est la 'reconsti-tution,' en Guinée et au Mali, d'une version canonique et consensuelle d'un texte de lois pluriséculaire ayant valeur de Constitution orale. Récupérée par les élites politiques ou culturelles, la Charte de Kurukan Fuga, telle qu'elle est figée par écrit en 1998, est en effet un épisode de l'épopée de Sunjata sciemment adapté au présent et à la 'modernité' par un collège panafricain de 'traditionnistes,' de juristes et de 'communicateurs.' Entérinée successivement par une conférence internationale organisée en 2004 à Bamako, puis par une publication collective en 2008, cette actualisation d'un récit épique, de son contenu à ses modalités d'énonciation, prend ici une forme inédite, mais cette énième transformation tex-tuelle et contextuelle de l'épopée n'en reste pas moins, aujourd'hui comme hier, l'expression de nouvelles revendications politiques et identitaires."

24. Mansare literally means "child of king."

25. To this day, the socio-historical region of Mande exists, and its denizens take pride in belonging to an unbroken line of Mandenka/Maninka indigenous to the area since pre-Sunjata times. The region lies across the borders of modern-day Mali and Guinea, mostly between Koulikoro (Mali) and Kankan (Guinea).

26. Jolly, 2010, pp. 901–2: "Aux yeux de ses producteurs ou de ses utilisateurs, ce texte, s'il trouve sa source dans un passé lointain et prestigieux, est moins une chronique historique qu'un manifeste politique, un code juridique ou une Constitution ayant valeur de modèle pour le présent, à une échelle nationale et panafricaine."

27. Most notably the Gana Empire, spanning across modern-day Mali and Mauritania.

28. In 2012, the story of "The Richest Man of All Time" was globally rediscovered, as Mali was struck by its worst crisis since the independence. Baby, M. (July 17, 2013). Thirteen raisons pour élire IBK en 2013. Retrieved from http://malijet.com/actualite-politique-au-mali/76971-mahamane-baby-13-raisons-pour-elire-ibk-en-2013.html.

29. He is of griot background.

Chapter 3

Birthing and Updating Narratives

MOBILIZING AN ANCIENT MALI FOR A NEW MALI

It should be noted that over the years, the Epic of Mande has seeped into all aspects of the media in Mali, as it has in the sister country of Guinea. After colonization ended, national radio (and television, later on) broadcasts were often set to the tune of episodes of the Epic of Mande. The voice of famed griot Bazoumana Sissoko resounded every day during the first decades after the Malian national radio started broadcasting. Songstresses of Mande tradition became officiants of major ceremonies held by the state.

Since the middle of the 1990s, this trend has greatly changed, with more egalitarian diffusions, so as to account for the diversity of the country. Still, several generations of Malians came of age with the idea of a Mali whose archways are made of Mande fabric.

The fact that both the first and the second president of independent Mali were of direct Maninka extraction helped ensure that in social memory, this new Mali and that ancient Mali would seem to be reflections of one another. Praise-singers competed to gain favors for leaders of the nation, recounting illustrious ancestry and the legitimacy to rule. Modibo Keita, during his eight years of rule, was heralded as a liberator of the nation, a direct descendant of Sunjata Keyta. Moussa Traore, like all Traore, was sung of as the grandson[1] of the most ambitious and victorious Tiramakan Tarawele.[2]

It appears that in the mighty constellation of Malian national identity, all agreed that, truly, power belonged with Mande. As recently as in 2013, during the presidential elections campaign, the party of Ibrahim Boubacar Keita[3]—who was ultimately elected—employed his paternal lineage as one of "thirteen reasons to vote for IBK,"[4] implying that his allegedly being a direct descendant of Sunjata meant he was more fit than his opponent, Soumaila Cissé (an ethnic Songhay of Fula extraction) to rule.

Upon Keita's victory in the elections, going forward to his formal inauguration ceremony, Bamako, the capital city of Mali, echoed with singing and remembrance of how *"Fanga Segina Mande,"*[5] as though it undeniably is from Mande that rightful rule may flourish. The popular narrative was that IBK was Sunjata come again, brash, and strong, and firm. He was the man needed to bolster change in a broken country on the verge of failure, where marginal people had attempted to sabotage nationhood. The election of IBK was very much a reaffirmation of the unity of Mali, while propaganda against Cissé often mentioned that he did not speak Bamanan and that he was hawkish in defending his roots in the north of Mali.[6] IBK had massive popular support, was backed by the military, and had favors of the international community. He was a unifier.

The shadow of former president Amadou Toumani Touré also lingered during these times of elections, in identity-centered discourses. Touré was ousted by a coup d'état, a mere month before elections that were to end his two legal terms as president. Touré, a Fula from Mopti region in central Mali, is widely believed to be a Maabo,[7] or from some other nonruling caste. Contemporary politics were reinterpreted to assert that the downfall of Mali may be due to the people having given power to one unworthy of it because of his social status, unlike the scion of Mande, that is, President Ibrahim Boubacar Keita.

There have been attempts to conflate all major figures of the country of Mali with Mande, one way or another. One idea posits that the symbol of Mande decisively united all Malians, despite apparent heterogeneity. The cities of Timbuktu and Djenne, and the Songhay imperial line of Askia Muhammad, as well as sixteenth-century Fula rebel and King Koli Tengela,[8] exemplify this practice. Timbuktu is said to have been founded by Tamasheq, but it became a prominent town under Mande rule. Djenne is an ancient city on the River Niger, where various communities met and with which Bozo people's lore is greatly associated. Though its apex happened during Fula rule in latter centuries, it is also one such city that was bolstered by imperial Mande rule. Askia Muhammad is referred to as a "Sillanke"[9] in various texts. Academics having uncovered some evidence that his lineage may be descended from the "Silla" patronymic clans from the ancient Old Gana Empire. He is made to appear more and more as an offshoot of Mande greatness. Koli Tengella was a warrior-hero from Kingi, in the Western Sahel.[10] His father, Tengela, of Ba patronym (one of the four classical patronyms of Fula people) rebelled against central imperial Songhay rule in the late fifteenth century because of oppressions against nomadic communities such as his. Tengela was called the "fake prophet of the Ful" due to the fervour of his followers and his charisma in stating the need for Fula to break free from imperial serfdom. Upon Tengela's death, Koli succeeded him and decided to invade Fuuta Tooro, in present-day Senegal and Mauritania, after fleeing to present-day Guinea to strengthen his troops. The life and deeds of Koli Tengela and his companions inspired a new grand epic.[11] Again, with the advancement of history and historiography, and with the combination of griot tradition with this advancement, it has now become widely accepted and taught that Koli Tengela was at least of half Maninka descent, through his mother's line. She is said to have been a Keyta, a direct descendant of Sunjata.[12] As such, Koli is retroactively anointed and legitimate to rule, possessing imperial Mande blood in him.

It is relevant to cite the example of Xaaso[13] as well. In the seventeenth century, through a cunning phenomenon, Fula invaders, upon deposing their Maninka overlords, took the tile of *"Mansa"*[14] to better rule among Maninka. In choosing a Maninka title of domination, they asserted themselves as followers of a line of rightful rule. Again, the idea that lingers is that "to properly rule, you must don the attributes of Mande." This was in a time far from now and far from the times of the Mali Empire.

We observe that the shaping of community narratives in Mali has been a continuous process for centuries. This very observation may bring some nuance to polarized discourses about the specifically contemporary nature of manipulation by current political elites. Still, it does draw a picture of non-negotiation and non-mitigation of Maninka supremacy over the centuries.

Jolly (2010) proposes that phenomena like the modern Malian Kurukan Fuga have contributed to an overall attempt by local elites to legitimize administrative decentralization by tapping into the Epic of Mande's sharing of power. In this understanding, Sunjata and his contemporaries set good practices for ruling in a vast realm. At a time when rebellions and weak government presence questioned the sustainability of Mali's existence, there was no question that the country's future would have to rethink the unitary mode of rule inherited from French colonization. France, as it appeared in its colonial dominions, pushed for a centralized unitary mode of direct rule to better exert control over peoples and resources. Even as African colonies were divided into multiple entities, their spaces remained vast and their day-to-day rule was upheld by distant leaders. In French Sudan, the French were represented by a governor who sat in the final capital, Bamako, atop the hill of Koulouba, "the hill of power." To this day, that is where the presidential palace lies—a massive picturesque building of "Soudanais style."[15]

Still, enduring through colonization, ancient Epics of Mande were reborn as symbols of freedom that could be universally employed.

A LAND OF HEROES, BLESSED BY GOD?

In addition to Great Mande, other symbols have joined the grand narrative of Mali as a nation. They diverge from the Mande narrative by several points. Mainly, these ideas have taken root over the ages, and they touch upon the very nature of the land and its people.

When ousted prime minister Cheick Modibo Diarra[16] declared on national television about Mali: "*Mali, nin dugu barikama!*,"[17] he seems to be simply stating what many think. This says a great deal about the immense trauma that were the events of 2012 and how Malians were trying to cling to deep cultural and group devices to garner hope. Many politicians and media commentators have voiced this same idea of Mali being a blessed country, incapable of sinking. This is the same idea that was ridiculed online by supporters of the Tamasheq rebels for whom Mali was a decadent country that failed them. A blessed Mali could only be a lie and a joke, then. Regardless of political alignment, it seems all loyalists could agree that Mali would rise from its ashes and that turmoil was the anomaly. Rebels, on the other hand, viewed the crisis as a revelator of what Mali truly was: a cracked shell under the veneer of greatness. How could they say otherwise? They were denying an invasive narrative they felt they were excluded from: that of Great Mande. Sullying Mali was not sullying themselves, for they had their own narratives of greatness, their own idols and pantheons.

One element that contributes to Mali's greatness and its hallowed status is the great number of heroic acts and sacred heroes it has known. As much as social memory is imprecise about dates and specifics of events, it does hold on to emotionally charged events.

To illustrate with a Fula example, we will recount a discussion we had in March 2013 with a native of Kayes.[18] We were talking about revisionism in Mali who[19] confided that having gone to school in Mali in her childhood, she always found it strange that Umar Tal[20] was taught at school to be a great hero and a staunch opponent of colonialism, while in her family's hometown, elders would go on about the crimes he committed in the area. These elders were not born yet during the times of the Umarian Jihad,[21] but they lived with people who had. Also, as with oral traditions and tales of griots, time appears as if it is compressed. At the time of the story she recounted, Umar Tal was waging a war that had killed denizens of the area by the hundreds. In her hometown, a story did the rounds that Umar Tal, upon a chance encounter with local Fula herders, asked them to help his troops cross a shallow but tricky body of water. Before the might of the ferocious *Nelaaɗo Alla*,[22] the herders agreed to show him how to safely cross over. They went on with their cattle, and once on the other side of the stream, they showed the right spots to tread on. They had actually managed to outsmart the Umarian troops, and many soldiers are said to have died on that day. The account goes that Umar became so furious he cursed the whole village. The person who shared this account claimed that to this day people from her village are said to be very temperamental and to argue with each other so much that few illustrious families remain and many have to eventually leave the village at one point or another. We both mused about how little importance was given to such depictions of Umar Tal in national narratives.

Robinson's work[23] frequently points out, social memory does not necessarily keep objective track of all shades of all narratives. In the case of jihads past, there exists, nowadays, a trend to romanticize them. Many a scholar, civil society actor, or politician, has backed the idea that jihads of the past were righteous and benevolent enterprises. Namely, the Umarian Jihad is glorified. Robinson, Tyam, and Gaden (1931) paint a different picture, with descriptions of horrors. Tyam, a religious scholar and contemporary loyal supporter of Umar during the times of the jihad, does not use pejorative language in recalling said horrors. He describes the struggle and the bloody victories perpetrated by his liege as sacred acts. This provides quite an interesting perspective when put back to back with Robinson's rigorously objective depictions of the harm done in Bamanan or Maninka countries of the Western Sudan. Robinson's explanations of dissatisfaction in the ranks of Umar's troops asserts just how even within the in-group negative feelings lingered. Almost two centuries later, group memory of descendants[24] of the Umarian movement utilizes the grand narrative of the "Umarian Epic" to recall greatness and pride. This occasionally extends to other Fula who sometimes do not know that their homelands were ravaged by Umarian troops. They praise Umar as a great Fula hero and appropriate perceived greatness when facing non-Fula. On a listserv of Fula diasporas, we suggested that Fula organizations acknowledge the heterogeneity of Fula memories and how grief about the Umarian war still existed. An elder from Maasina, one of those Fula polities attacked by Umar Tal, said that we should forget about past dissension and focus on future unity. In smaller groups, people were more vocal about their distaste for the Umarian Epic, but in larger settings and when facing non-Fula groups, Umar Tal was appropriated yet again.

Colonization was a dividing agent, aiming to conquer. And so it did. And in doing so, the local colonial superpower, France, paradoxically united native peoples of Mali around social memory. France maneuvered to depose former kings, to replace them with rival factions, and to ultimately topple whole indigenous social and political structures. Ultimately, it became evident that Europeans sought only to earn profit from their time in the region and its occupation.

Narratives may touch upon locations, too. Much has been said and done to assert that terrorism in Mali is a profound crime against its ancient and rich culture. That is why the city had to be protected. It holds an eclectic and inclusive value for all major community groups of Mali. Timbuktu epitomizes the strife about protecting Mali's heritage and religious secularism. The city holds a reputation for being a location of ancient cosmopolitan culture. Both the Tarikh Al Sudan and the Tarikh Al Fattash[25] depict the treasure trove it was for intellectuals. The city is known as the Mysterious City, the City of the 333 Saints, because of that same tradition of knowledge and mysticism. Timbuktu has attracted travelers and adventurers over the ages. The city reached its peak of fame between the fourteenth and the seventeenth centuries. In 1988, it was inducted into the UNESCO's World Heritage list. As such, after Timbuktu was occupied in 2012 by jihadist movements, the site attracted massive interest. This was the famed City of the 333 Saints, the city that had belonged to the Mande, Tamasheq, Songhay, Moroccans and Malian Arabs, Maasina Fula, and Fuuta Tooro Fula. Timbuktu is by far and large the most famed and famous city of Mali. Its fame and history have contributed to make it one of those sources of Mali's mystical protection in narratives of "Great Mali."

National narratives in Mali have tended to integrate and absorb as many local heroes as possible, contributing to a grand feat of inclusivity and rationalization. The constellation of Malian heroes who protected the country is quite bright as a consequence of this. From the times of primary school,[26] Malians learn of the great fights of their ancestors against colonial penetration and how colonizers pitted petty kings against each other to better rule.[27] With that vision, any leader who fought against the French invaders, no matter their creeds or reasons, are considered heroes of anti-colonialism. This extends to Firhoun Ag Alinsar, the last great rebel fighter of colonization according to official textbooks. This Tamasheq nobleman led the last episode of resistance until his death in 1924 and the pacification of the whole country—though faraway desert provinces were arguably never truly governed due to their remoteness[28] (a trend that would carry over to the Malian state after independence). Firhoun did not have any grand plan of resistance in the name of all of Mali. He was fighting for the preservation of his homeland in the north of Mali, along with a composite band of fighters from various communities.[29] While it is true that Firhoun raised the banner of Islam and declared a holy war against colonizers, this appears to have been a strategy to rally all peoples of his homeland under his coalition. It may seem somewhat paradoxical that Firhoun—the last of the greatest—comes from the people that was among the first to be subjected to the fires of Malian nationalism after 1960. However, it can be argued that the newly born Malian state did not specifically have an anti-Tamasheq agenda. Rather, in building the state, the forefathers of Mali had in mind to level the field and make all appear equal in the national narrative, and subject all peoples of Mali to a unitary, albeit totalitarian state.

The new state of Mali inherited the violence and the oppressive centralized commandment of colonial French Sudan. During the times of colonization, Tamasheq people mercilessly fought because of the difficulty of colonial authorities to hold them in check and manage their homelands.

BROKERING TERRITORY AND NATIONAL IDENTITY

Ideas of Malians needing to heed patriarchal leaders versus voicing dissent both appear nowadays in discussions about the elasticity of the Malian republic. Is the Malian republic a work in the making? Or is it set and fixed, with little possibility of pouring into nation-building anything that was not ordained by the political powers that be, namely the very Mande-adjacent rulers of the country? Through this perspective, Tamasheq rebellions have been proposing a real revolution in the way that Mali has been made to confront its national policymaking. By entirely questioning the veracity of the Mande epic and the values it allegedly brought into nation-building, rebels proposed alternative views of what it means to decide to be together. Confronting the inadequacies of Mali's discourse about itself as a pluralistic country, they brought with their rebellions an all or nothing take on coexistence. Either the state of Mali would accommodate their demands in terms of development, culture, and self-administration, or they would terminate the alliance into Mali. While it is certainly true that the rebels were not able to pursue a debate about these choices, the ultimate resolution of the violent conflict that opposed them with the state of Mali (with the help of the United Nations and international mediation) acknowledged the aspirations of the rebels to fully exist within Mali with more decentralized power from Bamako. Although it may seem that the Algiers agreements of 2015 solely pertained to the northern regions of Mali, their spirit aimed at broader reforms within Mali. The United Nations mission in Mali, the MINUSMA was designed to support efforts from the government to apply the spirit of the Algiers agreements,[30] in addition to its initial mandates of protection of civilians. As war seemed to abate, national narratives could be made great again.

President Ibrahim Boubacar Keita, after his accession to presidency, notably referenced the imperial past of Mali during a speech that became highly commented on the Internet, ironizing about the current decadence of Mali when an intangible memory of its past was still very much employed by politicians. President IBK declared at a maritime summit that *"Before others were, we were maritime country."*[31] He compared Mali favorably to other lands that never attained such early greatness. This became a social media memetic phenomenon as the press pointed out that Mali, a landlocked country, could hardly claim any such past marvel when it was currently so far away from the ocean and so dependent on neighboring maritime countries. This boast by the president appeared like a then too-usual general discourse aggrandizing a failing Mali, as if to self-realize a prophecy of greatness, in perpetual optimism, making Mali a power by sheer force of its narratives.[32] Internet memes would begin with "*We were*," and they would iterate a self-aggrandizing claim about Mali.[33] This instance shows how contemporary Malians reappropriate nationalistic narratives to assuage anxieties and to deflect political public relations attacks. There seems to be an ability to take a step back from the field and weaponize discourses that are far removed from realities. We must slightly mitigate this ability, though, as cyberspaces are not representative of general social reaction to political narratives. Additionally, it cannot be stated categorically that general reactions were made with the awareness of political pride tactics at hand or that even in being aware of them people would be willing to engage in political debates. Besides, people could candidly use these tropes themselves. This is even truer in a context when national morale was declining, and there was a very strong need for national symbols that could unite. Yet in uniting the many, what to do with the few who are too aware yet that they are commodities in a political popularity market? And how about those few who would not identify with political narratives?

The plan for narrative-building is an aged one, though. There has been, since the times of colonization, a narrative about a continuous grand Malian destiny expressed by all the greatness that has been realized in the country. Decolonization in Mali, though it did not come with major bloody revolts, was plotted with a struggle for the affirmation of grandeur. The narrative for independence in Mali that was employed by past leaders was geared around the idea that Mali was taking back its greatness. After all, as previously stated, at the end of colonization, Mali was emerging as an ancient nation reborn. The initial project for independence was to give birth to a two-state federation: "The Federation of Mali." This polity was to be comprised of France's local social and intellectual jewel, Senegal, and the bountiful and massive land of French Sudan.

There exist abundant accounts about the failure of the federal project. The narrative harkens back to stereotypes about the Senegalese, and about the Malian leader of independence, Modibo Keita. In prelude to independence, Modibo Keita visited his counterpart Léopold Sédar Senghor, in Senegal. There, Keita was allegedly strong-armed into giving up prospects of a federation led by Mali. The story goes that the Senegalese, ever the rebellious and distrusted subjects, were being manipulated by France. France had produced a local elite that was quite vocal and integrated into French politics to some extent. Even today, it is not uncommon to hear of this alleged special bond between France and Senegal, though it is debatable how fair such bond could be. Recent events have added fuel to the notion, however. Senegalese president Macky Sall created a polemic when recalling the status of Senegal and its past relationships with France. In May 2018, Macky Sall was denounced because of a public statement saying that Senegal was favored by France even during imperial domination and exploitation. As a case in point, he gave the example of "Senegalese Tirailleurs,"[34] saying that among them, those from Senegal itself were better treated, and "even got desserts,"[35] unlike other African soldiers.

At the times of independence, Modibo Keita was in turn criticized with a famous declaration from President Senghor, saying that "Modibo, you are not Sunjata, and Mali is not Ancient Mali, it is a giant with feet of straw."[36] Mali's atavistic attempts to instill the idea of the legitimacy of ancient Mali as a rightful ruler of the region were noticed and pointed out as early as the late 1950s. Mali, as its leaders wished, would represent a unitary state with a united people, even in fantasy cultivated by visiting foreigners, in an attempt to assuage anxiety about the dislocation of a country with such bountiful culture to be consumed, and sophisticated peoples to discover.

Senegal did not accept dominion. It became autonomous and independent on its own. The idea of autonomy versus Jacobian centralization is still highly debated in Mali to this day. There are different understandings of what it is that autonomy exactly means. The idea of partition for Malian masses has created anxious stances about the prospect of territories ruling for themselves. Though decentralization had been a rising and popular plan until the putsch in 2012 and the rebel conquests, it was viewed with worry about further implications in terms of power management, in the post-2012 era, with rebels having appropriated the term. What then, of state capacity to negotiate between legitimate claims of decentralization and dangerous claims of autonomy and independence?

THE TURNING POINT IN 2012

The putsch in Bamako, in March 2012, was a turning point in the national narrative of Mali. Amadou Aya Sanogo, the leader of the junta proudly proclaimed on national television that he had never voted in his whole life, that the third republic[37] of Mali was an utter failure. Criticism of deposed president Amadou Toumani Touré's failed democratic regime did focus not only on Touré's mistakes but also on a total reassessment of the values that had been poured into the modernization of Mali. Sanogo called for a strong state, a strong army, and no discussions with rebels. This was without a doubt the stance of a new party concerned with keeping a status quo when it came to direct government rule over everyday matters, as a rule of the righteous and the competent. Sanogo deemed democratic regimes of the past to be highly incompetent. One of the first actions by the junta was the arrest of several former government officials and public figures in Mali, including bankers, political leaders, or civil society actors, as well as soldiers too close to the fallen regime. Afterward, murders, destruction of property, and financial crimes would come to mire the actions of the junta.[38] Its leaders, though, promoted the narrative that they were rebooting the country's system. The narrative that they offered warrants interest and consideration, too. It is a narrative that exacerbated nationalism and centered itself on unitary and militaristic ideas of what Mali should be. In this, the junta had been summoning a political culture that existed within the army since the times of colonization and more broadly into military culture of Mali in certain specific areas of the country.[39] For this reason, it has been necessary to have a look at the historical and cultural bases of the doctrine of the junta, and how that doctrine came to engage Malians and create new narratives and reactions that are still apparent today. The junta that committed the coup d'état hails from an institution (the Malian army) that is entrenched both in indigenous mores and colonial legacy of violence and militarism. Since Mali's independence, possessing an army has been an automatic tenet of the Malian state, and the structure of the Malian army was based on the colonial army. The first Malian officers were veterans of World War II, the Indochina War of Independence, and the Algeria War of Independence. They came from Indochina and Algeria with experience in torture and counterinsurgency. The brutal ways with which indigenous Asians and Africans who opposed the French Empire were dealt with were also used in Mali to combat indigenous Malians such as Tamasheq dissidents and civilians from their homelands.[40] Hence, the ideal Mali that was spoken of was impossible to accept for victims of the state and their families and friends.

"Mali never existed the way we were taught about it. Sunjata is a fairy tale and this country is based on it. No wonder it's failing so bad," as can be recalled from supporters of the MNLA Tamasheq rebellion. In a clear attempt to contest narratives of Mali that were hegemonic and that did not include them, online militants flooded discussions with ideas about Mali's failure as modern country to bring justice, development, and overall good governance to its citizens. Denying Mali's grandiose past, and even insulting it, usually took the result form of goading which in turn created escalations in affirmations of narratives and identities that did not deal in nuance: Grand Mali versus Grand Azawad, Tamasheq treason versus Malian incompetence, sub-Saharans versus Saharans, and so forth. In this zero sum game of confronted discourses, possibilities of sincere discussions, exchanges, and productive peacebuilding were sparse or completely absent. Conflict was demanded in order to reexamine festered wounds and achieve catharsis regardless of empathy for other parties which could not be viewed as co-participants, but only as antagonists. Differences in adhesion to narratives, then, represented opposition that was to be met with harshness. To defend narratives upon which they had been raised, staunch "loyalists" devalued any claims to Azawad's reality and to Tamasheq pride. Opposing them, defenders of Azawad seemed intent on destroying narratives that could bring credence to the idea that Mali as a country was sustainable still and that the rebellion may have been curtailed. In order to promote the agendas of the rebellion, Mali had to be dismantled as a fiction and a lie. Hence, representatives of the MNLA went on several media sets or exposed themselves on social media, explaining that Mali was a fake democracy, that there were no Malian people, that the international seduction of Mali was all style and no substance. There did not seem to be room for compromise nor for remembrance of shared history. Even figures such as Moussa Ag Assarid,[41] a Tamasheq writer and longtime activist for Tamasheq causes, no longer defended his identity as a Malian, when he used to.

This fall from grace was met not with introspection, but with hard nationalistic narratives. Even as Tamasheq rebels began to point to Bamako amid the drama of the March 2012 coup d'état, and say that this was proof that the house of cards was coming down and that they had been right, and the narrative of a strong eternal Mali endured in the country was all lies. We hypothesize that this was a defensive reaction to the fall of a country that had belonged with, and on whose survival and daily livelihood were thrust aside. In parallel, working as a volunteer psychologist in Mali, in 2012, we faced accounts of Malians from the south, expressing their fears of growing emotional illnesses because their world seemed to shatter. This was quite a new phenomenon. Having previously worked in Mali,[42] we were rarely heard Malians sharing feelings about emotional distress and mental illness about social events. Though it is impossible to generalize from scarce interviews, hardship seemed to have reached a level at which it was no longer possible to act stoically and to take in emotions without flinching. A civilian youth who used to live on a military base personally explained[43] to us that he felt traumatized by violence caused by both local (caused by the army, and which he experienced firsthand) and violence in the north.

Testing narratives they had always believed in was proving very difficult for Malians at the time. And they obviously did not get any compassion from supporters of the rebellion at a time when threats to the existence of Mali seemed dire in the south of the country because of the political chaos at the summit of statehood.

Since these days, a new narrative has become very popular: that of "The Big Malian Lie." As media pundits and politicians pointed out that Mali's model of democracy and its status as international community darling had been a sham, a social mental shift and readjustment was taking place, with growing dissent. From denial and clinging to olden ideas of a strong and ever-prosperous Mali, more and more Malians espoused the idea that Mali had really been a giant with feet of straw all along. Mali was a poor country. It was a country with dirty politicians. It was a land of spiritual corruption attacked by self-righteous jihadists. Movements based on religious purification, nationalist rebirth, community empowered, certainly were watered with the tears shed from disappointment in Mali's abilities to come through hardships. *Mali, nin dugu barikama ("Mali, this blessed land")*, in the words of Cheick Modibo Diarra, was not living up to its narrated and oversold blessings.

NOTES

1. In griot fashion, time is compressed, and deeds of ancestors, numerous though they may be, are told as if they had occurred in times of recent memory (Barry, 2011). This allows for a recuperation of features and feats of heroes past by present-day personages.

2. Tiramakan, one of the scions of the revolutionary epoch of Mande, possesses his own epic. He is famously remembered as the conqueror of various dependencies of Mande, among which the precious faraway lands by the River Gambia, all the way to the Atlantic Ocean.

3. Commonly known by his initials, IBK.

4. The author of this article, Mahamane Baby, is himself from the north of Mali, and he is a Malian Arab. It is quite telling that individuals outside of the Mande heartland would use the popularity and subconscious power of Mande narratives as an electoral tool, too. One may wonder about the consequences of such mass-spinning on identity-shaping in their native communities, most of all in times of duress. Baby, M. (July 17, 2013). 13 raisons pour élire IBK en 2013. Retrieved from http://malijet.com/actualite-politique-au-mali/76971-mahamane-baby-13-raisons-pour-elire-ibk-en-2013.html.

5. "Power has returned to Mande," in Bamanan.

6. Cissé does, in fact, speak perfect Bamanankan, and often makes a point to speak in Bamanankan as if to prove his "Malianness."

7. They are a courtesan-type caste of cloth weavers, in charge of holding ceremonial processions, and entertainment. They are considered to be one of the middle castes in Fula societies.

8. Kane, 2005. Some griots go as far as to say that Koli is the grandson of Sunjata who reigned three centuries before. In the epic of Koli, his mother is often cited as a Keyta, a "daughter of Sunjata."

9. Ba Konaré, 1977.

10. In Mali, the Western Sahel is the historical region along the southern border of Mauritania, stretching from Kayes Cercle and Nara Cercle.

11. The epic of Grand Fulo and the Deniyankooɓe is popular with griots of Senegal and Mauritania.

12. Some griots go as far as to say that Koli is the grandson of Sunjata who reigned three centuries before. In the epic of Koli, his mother is often cited as a Keyta, a "daughter of Sunjata."

13. Cissoko, 1986.

14. The title of rulers of the Mali Empire.

15. A colonial architectural style devised after French occupation began in the region.

16. "CMD" is a former NASA cadre. He built his popularity both on his credentials abroad and his roots in the Bamanan heartland, as a "child of Mali." In his own words, "Mali has given me everything, I have no choice but to stay on as prime minister" (televised allocution on July 29, 2012). Mali: Le Premier ministre refuse de démissionner et formera un gouvernement d'union nationale (July 29, 2012). Retrieved August 7, 2018, from http://koaci.com/m/mali-premier-ministre-refuse-de missionner-formera-gouvernement-d'union-nationale-76523-i.html.

17. In Bamanankan, this translates as "Mali, this blessed and protected country." Literally "Mali, this *Baraka*-infused country." *Baraka* is primarily an Islamic concept. In Mali, it is used to denote the status of protection granted by God to those he favors.

18. The first capital of French Sudan, in the westernmost part of Mali.

19. This was a candid discussion of the kind we enjoy, to get a measure of non-academics' views on political events, and how they position themselves with regards to current politics.

20. The Fula "armed prophet" who swept through the Western Sudan from his homeland Fuuta Tooro in present-day Senegal and Mauritania (Robinson, 1985).

21. Tal's holy war began in 1848 in present-day Guinea, at the margins of the Fula Theocratic Empire of Fuuta Jaloo, and with the support of its leaders. He died in present-day Mali in 1864. His heirs went on to conquer more lands in that part of the Sudan.

22. *The Messenger* of God. This was one of the titles Umar Tal was praised with, from the times of his holy war.

23. Robinson, 1985.

24. We ourselves have ancestors on both family lines, among who Tyam. Many came as scholars, others came as warlords, some came on foot or riding cattle. All came because of the call of the *Messenger* to conquer new lands where faith would create a better life. As such, the Umarian Epic is recounted as a tale of resettlement and glory, though it ultimately ended with internal struggles and betrayals, during the advent of colonial France in the region. It extends from a tradition of Fula mass exodus called *fergo*, similarly to the conquest of Xaaso.

25. Arab language African sources favored by historians.

26. Namely, in the sixth year of school. A thorough overview of Malian political history is taught to students. The course starts from the empire of Gana, and goes on beyond the times of independence. The focus is set on great dates and greats peoples, with a general description of events. There are four major parts in this curriculum: the times of the great empires, smaller kingdoms and colonial penetration, independence, modern era.

27. This narrative dates back to the times of independence, when the socialist state tried to solidify the foundation of Mali as a nation-state, a united polity with an unbreakable reason to exist.

28. Ba Konaré & Konaré, 1983.

29. Notably, Fula and Songhay fought for Firhoun, and many of them, upon defeat, were deported to the neighboring French colony of Guinea until the end of their lives (Grémont, 2005).

30. During a Global Forum Meeting in Paris on June 9, 2015, former Burundi president Pierre Buyoya, as the high-representative of the MISahel, thoroughly explained the Algiers Agreements. They were to be taken as a foundation for cooperation between the Malian government and Tamasheq rebel movements. The final text would dissatisfy all parties, but it was meant to convey a general spirit of cooperation between all parties, as moral agreement going beyond written words.

31. Lomé, Togo, October 18, 2016. "Avant que d'autres ne le fussent, nous fûmes un pays maritime !" : Chronique satirique: L'amiral Ladji Bourama au sommet sur la sécurité maritime (October 18, 2016). Retrieved from https://bamada.net/chronique-satirique-lamiral-ladji-bourama-au-sommet-sur-la-securite-maritime.

32. Imperial Mali did have access to the ocean through its conquests. This goes on to reinforce the notion that present-day Mali is a successor of ancient Mali.

33. *"We were rulers of the world before other were,"* *"We conquered Africa before others did,"* and so on.

34. This term remains a misnomer as all West African troops fighting in France's colonial armies during their international campaigns were called "Tirailleurs Sénégalais." This is telling of the status of Senegal as a base for French operations in Africa. Senegal was indeed among the first lands settled in sub-Saharan Africa by France, most notably with coastal trading posts as early as the seventeenth century, some two centuries before colonial expansion in the region.

35. AFP (May 28, 2018). Au Sénégal, le président Macky Sall accusé d'avoir" insulté la mémoire des tirailleurs." Retrieved from https://www.lemonde.fr/afrique/article/2018/05/28/au-senegal-le-president-macky-sall-accuse-d-avoir-insulte-la-memoire-des-tirailleurs_5305963_3212.html.

36. This radio source was cited by several elders in Mali—people who lived at the times of independence and still remembered it. However, we were never able to find formal sources citing it.

37. Mali has been in the third chapter of its republican endeavours, since the advent of democracy in 1992, after dictator Moussa Traoré was toppled in 1991.

38. Human Rights Watch has been relentless in covering atrocities committed in Mali by all parties: government forces, the military junta, and non-state armed groups. World Report 2013: Rights Trends in World Report 2013: Mali (February 7, 2013). Retrieved from https://www.hrw.org/world-report/2013/country-chapters/mali.

39. Northern regions of Mali, distant and unruly, were dealt with using extreme prejudice since the times of colonization (Ba Konaré & Konaré, 1983).

40. Interview with a retired Malian officer in May 2012.

41. La situation sécuritaire au Nord en débat sur TV5: Chaudes empoignades entre Chato et Moussa Ag Assarid (December 17, 2012). Retrieved from http://bamada.n

et/la-situation-securitaire-au-nord-en-debat-sur-tv5-chaudes-empoignades-entre-chato-et-moussa-ag-assarid.

42. We hold a doctorate degree in clinical psychology, and we were working as a psychologist at a public hospital in Mali at the time of research for our dissertation, in 2011 and 2012.

43. Bamako, May 2012.

Chapter 4

Clashing Episodes in Fula Narratives

A TECHNOLOGICAL REVOLUTION IN NARRATION

With war in the north of Mali and failed attempts at regulating security in other parts of Mali, communities of central Mali began to grow anxious about their future, too. Jihadist groups extended their area of influence, and community militias gradually appeared. In order to protect themselves or to support the aspirations of their communities, various groups banded together during the years of this study (2012–2018) and took up arms. Each band has been defending narratives that come into direct clash with each other. The revolution of Information and Communications Technology (ICT) has made it much easier to connect people. Contrarily to what many observers presume, it is actually not difficult to communicate with people in the hinterland, or even with mobile communities. Hearing religious scholars preach, getting pictures of massacres, and finding out about the whereabouts of displaced relatives have all become basic realities of everyday news. In all areas of Mali, it is possible to get access to mobile phone networks and receive information.[1] Even at the apex of the Malian crisis in 2012–2013, denizens of Mali were able to communicate about events unfolding. Facebook became a prime source of information, as well as WhatsApp phone group chats. Even researchers (including ourselves), usually won't be suspicious of Internet posts, started to analyze speech and content provided by Internet users. Though very hard to discriminate between fake propaganda-aimed profiles and genuine users, social media has been constantly providing trends about all arrays of ideas, fears, expectations, and emotions. After a few hours visiting Facebook groups, trends become apparent. Data saturation can be easily reached: we may witness a display of all that it is possible to hear, though quantitative data is imprecise. This does not mean that allegiances expressed and observed thusly are proportionate to allegiances in the field. It does paint a picture of the many nuances available. The harder and more passionate part of such research is to be capable to differentiate sources according to their reliability.

On a more functional and mundane aspect, Internet-based ways of communicating created platforms for self-narration and dissemination of daily matters. Phoning apps such as WhatsApp or Signal have become very popular in all parts of Mali. Communities create thousands of groups, each with hundreds of members. Therein, they post pictures, audio messages, text, and so on. With this, even isolated people get some sort of daily news, flavored with the identity and spirit of the group they are members of. It is possible to find primary sources through such networks and to locate dangerous locations as well. These tools, while useful, can be used for dissemination of fake news and to rile up masses for specific political agendas. Images and audio messages from other parts of Africa are candidly or maliciously shared. Sometimes, the intent is to sow fear. Other times, it is meant to reinforce group solidarity and aggressiveness.

As such, they are prime variables of the efficiency of narratives. They cannot be overlooked in gathering and analyzing data on popular narratives, their impacts, and their evolution. For instance, we have observed in Fula groups a trend to recall victimization of Fula and their alleged state of martyrs everywhere they live in Africa. Tears fuel anger, as they destroy morale. Victimization may induce a mass group reaction of sadness and apathy, as it can be weaponized. We have firsthand witnessed instances of call to arms and violent retribution with extreme prejudice, as we have witnessed activists and laypersons lose motivation and veer into depressive states.

The power of new technologies is a double-edged sword. Depending on who, how, and to what extent, and to what intent they are used, they could change the future in the field. With targeted publications on social, nowadays, it is possible to promote highly impactful information and to access precisely targeted communities as far away as in remote villages and anywhere Internet networks function.

UNRELENTING TENSIONS BETWEEN NEIGHBORS IN THE "DOGON COUNTRY"

What is referred to as the Dogon Country is an area located in the center of Mali, exclusively in Mopti region. The Dogon Country stretches over the Cercles of Bandiagara, Bankass, Koro, and Douentza.

Geographically, this is an area of plains and hills. Agriculture is the main activity of Dogon, as fishing is for Bozo[2] in the area, and cattle herding for

Fula. Religious teaching, though less exclusive, was traditionally the domain of Fula as well, for historical reasons. This is due to the jihad of Seku Amadu, in Macina, at the beginning of the nineteenth century. It was a major wave of conversion in the area, until the armies of Umar Tal toppled their Macina Fula kinsmen's rule in their very own jihad. Islam rested in the hands of Fula scholars, mostly.³

Social memory in the Dogon Country is rife with tensions regarding interethnic relations. In addition to anthropological accounts of the trauma inflicted by Fula conquerors in this land, there lingers in the words of Dogon organizations vying for the advancement of their homeland some bitterness about how to deal with Fula. In our experience, this is visible in interaction attempts between Fula civil organizations and Dogon organizations, behind the curtains and beyond official apparent compromise. As of now, the two dominant organizations for each community are respectively Tabital Pulaaku Mali,⁴ and Gina Dogon.⁵ In the local Fula tongue, Fulfulde, Dogon are referred to as "Humbeɓe" or "Haaɓe."⁶ Similarly, Bozo, the people of the river, are sometimes referred to as "*Sebɓe*."⁷ Both these terms exist with other employs elsewhere in the Fula nation. There still exists a prevalent idea that Fula hold a superiority complex toward all other peoples, and mostly toward those they ruled in the past.

Auno Guindo, a bard from the Dogon Country, has popularized the idea that Dogon are descended from a people who had come from Mande, the setting of the epic of Sunjata Keyta, the legendary founder of the Mali Empire. Jolly (2010) explains how this serves to ensconce Dogon into a national narrative in which they belong to Malian national narratives, and in which they are not marginal but kin to central actors. Thus, Dogon may elevate their externally perceived status from remote peasants to scions of ancient Mali. In the 1990s, Dogon identity was promoted within Mali. Jolly attributes the rise of particular versions of epics and history to the appearance of new modes of communication. Radio Seno, created in 1994, was a powerful driving force in the acquisition of knowledge about community history by Dogon. Bards, storytellers, griots from the region promoted stories and narratives to eager audiences. Outside of ceremonial declamations, in a context of special ordered recitals, bards would use their skills to bring forth narratives that were sure to entertain and ingratiate listeners, notably with a style of chanting known as the *baji kan*.⁸ Thus, Dogon are presented as one of the great peoples of Mali. This is of major importance since Dogon' main rivals in these lands, Fula, with their high number, exuberant history, and presence throughout Africa, seemingly held more prestigious narratives in popular majority social and mental representations. In the past, Fula herders, in establishing hegemonic ethnocentric and theocratic kingdoms, ruled over the pagan Dogon and marginalized them. It is often mentioned that a lot of the current tensions between Dogon and Fula stems from resentment over history and social memory. We believe this to be a far too conveniently simple explanation, all the more when one considers peaceful coexistence that was sometimes possible between these two peoples. The golden era of Dogon Country tourism did benefit all communities. In the 1990s and the early 2000s, thousands of tourists would annually visit central Mali and contribute to the renown and the sustainability of local communities. They would come from all around the world. The marvelous natural wonder of the hills and the drylands allowed herders, farmers, craftsmen, and fisherfolks, to make a livelihood and to connect with foreigners. Between 2012 and 2018, however, the joys of those times were little heard of. Antagonism is strong. Some Dogon militant groups have been using the history of Fula imperialisms as an argument to justify their mistrust of Fula folks and the dangers of leaving power in Fula hands. This started on Facebook pages and WhatsApp groups. Surely, there are multiple factors at play in tensions between Fula and Dogon. To cite a few, there is fighting for the use of lands and greenery, democratic political stakes, economic competition over ownership and commercialization of cattle, and so on. Responding to calls by Fula-originating organizations to protect Fula cultures, allegedly opposing activists in the media and on social networks have been promoting the idea of a unified and strong "Dogon Country." Namely, the group "Dogon Vision" purported to propose a plan for the development of the region around major Dogon cities. However, his plan seems to be failing in giving space to other communities, even beside Fula neighbors. In the current civil war context, there has been little hope for any form of sustainable and prolonged development as long as violence has not been curtailed. And so, in the meantime, discourses about strengthening local geopolitical identities appeared to play a role only in hardening bilateral stances about intercommunity relations.

Though it is hard to empirically evaluate the degree to which masses subscribe to this renewed hawkish identity claim, it is easy to observe counter-reactions from one main type of rival: Fula organizations. The dynamics between Fula organizations and Dogon organizations seem cordial in appearance. But in Internet forums of both communities, polarized discourses are omnipresent. To dismiss discourses and historical narratives from Dogon that would deny them rights to the land, some Fula have been proposing discourses and narratives of their own that discredit Dogon claims to the area. One such rests on Dogon's very own prestige narratives about their own arrival in the hills of the Dogon Country. If one accepts that Dogon are latecomers from Mande and that they replaced already-thriving communities in their current homeland, then their absolute claim to the region appears as weak as Fula's. Fula people, because of their later dominion and the widespread use of their language, and because of their seemingly stronger numbers in Mali, have had an advantageous vantage point to deconstruct Dogon narratives since the early nineteenth century.

THE TAMASHEQ REDEFINING NARRATIVES

The MNLA[9] was born in 2011 as an organization seeking to advocate for the Tamasheq of northern Mali. The MNLA began its first armed operations in January 2012, when it participated in the attack of Menaka, in northeastern Mali. The MNLA innovated from the experience of past Tamasheq rebellions. In their public relations plans, they initially insisted on expressing that they had the interests of all peoples of what they called the Azawad at heart. However, a history of mass violence in northern Mali both by state actors and by non-state belligerents, such as Tamasheq rebel groups and militias from other communities reacting to rebel attacks, fostered a climate of distrust such that the MNLA did not earn any sizeable support from neighboring communities when they claimed to be advocating for them and for their representation within the state of Mali. The MNLA's endeavors very much appeared to be attempts to enlist support for Tamasheq-centered agendas. After all, the timeline of the MNLA's existence was deeply rooted in the legacy of recent strife between Tamasheq groups and the state of Mali. In 2006, an agreement was signed in Algiers[10] under Algerian leadership. Tamasheq rebels had taken up arms to denounce the lack of development and infrastructures in their secluded regions despite commitments by Malian governments and pledges by the international community. With the growing presence of Al-Qaeda-affiliated armed fundamentalist Islamic groups, insecurity became a major issue in northern Mali. The Algiers Agreements of 2006 meant the Malian government would give more leeway to armed groups native to the area to defend their claimed territories. This was a new take on the claims of Tamasheq groups on those areas they deemed to be their homelands. The Malian army would be retreating from these areas outside of its effective control, maintaining bases in key cities only. De facto armed groups, along with the Algerian army, were in charge. As such, as violent Islamic fundamentalism grew in the area, and kidnappings of foreigners became frequent. Tamasheq groups gained specialization as middle-agents and brokers for the release of hostages. The gap left by Mali in terms of security and legitimacy helped embolden the sentiment of legitimacy by Tamasheq groups with the idea that the state of Mali was deficient and no longer a reliable ruler.

When denunciation of living conditions grew in the Tamasheq civil society in 2011, public opinion leaders in other communities of Mali began to take umbrage and to fear another rebellion might be in the making. Facing popular unrest, the Malian government took what were surely populist and largely symbolic measures to tame the situation. This did not result in any major policy change with regards to the development of the north of the country, nor any major change in doctrine or even strategy when operating in the north. What amounted to seemingly superficial decisions proved to have dramatic and lasting consequences. The state of Mali operated a crackdown on those organizations that were hardly threatening. Militants of then MNA were arrested, with some of them manhandled. Beyond human rights concerns this drew, it brought arguments for militants to point out that Mali was now past discussing with and that the next course of action was taking up arms to change the power balance.

During an interview we held with former MNLA leader, Moussa Ag Acharatoumane in 2015, he told us: "At first, I was just a student and then I became a militant. By brutalizing us, the Malian government made me a rebel, and then I became a military commander. My circumstances changed entirely." This narrative of progression and radicalization in advocacy became the standard story told in the media, even after peace was sought between rebels in Mali. However, recent interviews with individuals linked to the MNA and the MNLA have revealed that the plan had been to begin a rebellion all along. There had been a realization since the early 2000s that Bamako, under the rule of President Amadou Toumani Touré, would never satisfy the demands of Tamasheq organizations. Tamasheq elites in government were deemed inefficient and unreliable. Thus, a line was drawn between Malian government loyalists and rebellion sympathizers within Tamasheq societies. One fighter of that time told us in no uncertain terms that the plan was to create military[11] conditions for an uprising then stall so that a political bureau could mature.

The arrival of Libyan returnees in 2011, after the fall of Muammar Gaddafi accelerated the process of the great Tamasheq uprising. These returnees brought with them not only weapons but also determination, leadership, and military capability. Early skirmishes with the Malian army in a terrain they were quite familiar with allowed them to loot military material. At one point, rebel leaders declared that the majority of their equipment had come from the Malian army's arsenal, boasting an ability to both win battles and equip themselves to further their new agenda: partition and separatism. The north of Mali, which they called Azawad,[12] was rightfully theirs, and they had the means to administer and defend it against both terrorist armed groups and Malian institutions.[13]

Part of the MNLA's narrative for rebellion focused on their inclusion of all peoples of Azawad. They claimed to not solely represent Tamasheq aspirations, so as to garner wider local and international support. They communicated on development and security issues, as well as the murky relationships between Malian rulers and drug cartels and Islamic fundamentalist groups, proposing a partition that would allow them to focus on the prosperity of their own regions. In communicating about their ambitions, the rebels insisted on not being concerned with politics of the south of Mali.[14]

They deemed their territory to be the unified sum of the three regions of the north of the country: Timbuktu region, Gao region, and Kidal region. The choice of these regions was tactical, in order to maintain attention on a specific semi-arid and arid region already known for its rough environment. However, with many Tamasheq being of nomadic tradition, some communities would sometimes travel and settle as far south as Mopti region and Ségou region. This new Tamasheq nationalism tried to standardize what it was to belong to their community and identity around a territory where its proponents felt they could stand their ground and realistically defend ideas of partition. The desert was viewed as their dominion. So, they could claim the desert and rationalize their narrative by claiming to be its masters. We posit that going beyond the desert would appear to be overreaching and going beyond credible narrative. The narrative of being the true guardians of the desert damaged relationships with other denizens of the north, though. Moreover, the MNLA's ways might have seemed very appealing in a time when jihadism held a quasi-monopoly on world attention for North Africa and the Sahel. The MNLA's narrative truly had diverse elements to make it sympathetic and to get the support they needed: international support. Local support, though useful, was not and could not be the endgame in a fight that would be long and costly, unlike support from powerful external allies. Neighboring communities in the area the MNLA viewed as its dominion did not respond well to the attempts of the rebels to speak in their names. Other Tamasheq organizations tried to strike at the narrative of the MNLA. They spoke up about the need to unite under the same national banner, to follow democratic mores, to recognize the hardships of development in other faraway provinces of Mali, to take internal responsibility for the failure of development in the north. Former prime minister Ahmed Mohamed Ag Hamani was intent on dissociating the MNLA from the general Tamasheq public opinion.

The MNLA had decided that the communities of Azawad were Tamasheq, Arab, Songhay, and Fula. Sometimes, Dogon and Bozo, denizens of the region of Mopti, at the borders of Azawad, were included. Douentza Cercle and Youwarou Cercle (both in Mopti region) were occupied by rebels and their allies, too. Hence, the peoples there, though not part of the four main peoples, were components of Azawad at times, in discourses. It remains difficult to know whether specific strategies were aimed at these peoples.

Across the border, in neighboring Niger, the success of the MNLA's rebellion was feared by the government, as scarce chatter indicated that some ethnic Tamasheq from Niger also called for a broader Tamasheq front the union of all Tamasheq spaces. This would have been a weakening factor in the MNLA's strategy. Though the aspirations of fellow Tamasheq fit into the same narrative of injustice and revolution espoused by the MNLA, they did not possess in Niger the tactical elements they had nourished in Mali. And so, incursions into Niger could have weakened both their military strength, and their unity, since the international community had been responding well to their narrative so far. Mali experienced a coup d'état in March 2012. Niger was then more stable than Mali, and local authorities tried to placate Tamasheq in ostentatious ways. It would not do well to wage a war that would break the momentum the MNLA had been able to seize and disseminate all over the world, with their military success, their media smashes, their web-activism.

The narrating strategy forged by the MNLA may be described "total," because of the multifaceted ways it relied on: The Internet, politics, the media, and so on. This was very much an opportunity born from the global world and its tools for communication, for movement, for exchange.

Some victims of these events denounced an instrumentalization of their suffering by rebels, to this day. In a classic fashion, armed groups took a monopoly on denunciation, and civil society actors were not much capable of advocating in a way that was neither audible enough nor appealing enough. In February 2012, marches took place in Bamako, and protesters destroyed property owned by Tamasheq (including officials). Across the country, there were reports of Tamasheq being beaten, looted, and sometimes killed by angry citizens blaming them for the dislocation of Mali after the first successes of the MNLA. Some events were quite traumatic during the creation of the rebellion, and they became landmarks of the MNLA's narrative. The "pogroms" in Bamako,[15] in February 2012, and the flight of the "red-skinned" from Mali, is one unfortunate tragic episode that plotted on and fed into the MNLA's strategic narratives.

It is important to ponder the extent to which leaders of the MNLA's approach both toward other communities and toward reluctant Tamasheq was lip service and part of a tactic to ostentatiously showcase their willingness to cooperate with all, all the while focusing more discreetly on long-term non-populist war tactics. In the end, though, the MNLA's communication and recruitment tactics enabled them to make Mali stumble, and to get international traction for their cause.

NARRATING NEW ALLIANCES IN THE "WAR ON TERROR"

The impact of the times of occupation in 2012–2013 still lingers nowadays in community dynamics of Mali and in how power has been brokered.

In Bamako, since the onset of the crisis, successive governments have tried to garner support for themselves by defending the idea that the country's turmoil was an anomaly, a transient phenomenon caused by international terrorism. As armed groups gained power in northern Mali, starting from the massacre in Aguelhok (Kidal region) upon the fall of the army garrison and the execution of nearly one hundred soldiers at the hands of jihadist group Ansar Dine on January 24, 2012, it started to become clear that Tamasheq rebels who had vowed to now fight the central government with an irredentist agenda were not the only type of movement battling over lands and peoples. The MNLA made rebuttals about its responsibility. However, at the time of the massacre in Aguelhok[16] and several violent skirmishes, the MNLA was openly associated with Ansar Dine.[17] Ansar Dine was founded by Iyad Ag Ghaly, a longtime Tamasheq rebel leader, who was integrated and later became a political advisor in Bamako, and the consul of Mali in Saudi Arabia. The movement was made up of ethnic Tamasheq first and foremost. Its essential difference with the MNLA was that while the MNLA purported to fight for the advent of an independent Tamasheq state in northern Mali, Ansar Dine claimed to want to impose Sharia Islamic Law in northern Mali. Tribal alliances made it so that the MNLA, Ansar Dine, and Tamasheq returnees from Libya,[18] all being of Tamasheq extraction, allied in order to benefit from each other's expertise: political structure, tactical acumen, and weapons and ammunition. With that pool of expertise, the hope was that time would later come to divide the spoils of war among themselves. However, international attention and popularity for the MNLA required them to justify their actions in the field and clarify their alignments. With Ansar Dine appearing as the obvious leader of the Tamasheq coalition, and Iyad Ag Ghaly's support of international jihadism, dissentions appeared between allies. By June 2012, the Tamasheq coalition was in shambles and jihadist movements were stronger than ever. This is when the MUJWA rose and started confronting the MNLA on their turf. The MUJWA being more ethnically diverse, was less prone to follow tribal alliances and deals between Tamasheq groups.

Although the Tamasheq coalition never enjoyed much popularity in other communities of northern Mali, it had little to no credibility in the South. The coalition never won universal support from the Tamasheq civil in Bamako, but it was able to disseminate its symbols of nationalism (a government by the MNLA in occupied territories in the northern half of Mali's lands, and a flag) and narrate a story of righteous heroes rising to take their responsibilities to defend their community and bring about justice and righteousness in a land that was undoubtedly separate from corrupt Mali and its decaying power. The MNLA was swift in widening its missions to be inclusive of those communities they deemed to be the peoples of Azawad in addition to the Tamasheq: Arab, Songhay, and Fula. These four peoples were systematically introduced into all communications by the MNLA. Sometimes, Dogon and Bozo people were mentioned as well, when Azawad was viewed not only as the three regions from northern Mali, but as all the areas where Tamasheq people lived. Still, all government lists issued by the MNLA exhibited members that were almost all Tamasheq. Only a handful of members on lists of more than twenty people were Arab or Songhay.[19] Though of *Maïga*[20] patronym, Mahamadou Dieri Maïga, once the vice president of the MNLA, is widely associated with Tamasheq communities. Top leadership of the MNLA was always Tamasheq.

The narrative of an inclusive MNLA and a benevolent rebellion set on freeing peoples of northern Mali who they called their kin (as opposed to southern peoples who were deemed distant and foreign) never could become popular. The MNLA was decried, criticized, and opposed by leagues of northern associations throughout the times of the occupation of northern Mali by the Islamist coalition. Resentment against the MNLA was still vivid in 2018, more than five years since their rebellion began.

To further oppose the rebels, racist narratives were disseminated over social networks and made evident the ways in which social memory was deeply affected by the traumatic times of rebellions past. Just as the Malian army and self-defense militias are accused of having committed mass atrocities, Tamasheq rebels have been blamed for tragic human rights abuses ranging from theft to torture, murder, and rape. To reject Tamasheq claims to land and political power, narratives of Tamasheq "foreignness" were often summoned by activists wanting to discredit the rebellion. In so doing, Tamasheq memories of victimhood were trampled as well. Little regard was given to attachment to the name "Azawad" which was always only a Tamasheq word used in everyday life. On social media, opponents of the MNLA used the pun "Azamerde,"[21] antagonizing Tamasheq proponents of the term Azawad (pro-government and otherwise), and continuing a cycle of antagonization and mental violence.

It must seem quite the wonder that out of the coalition of rebels that opposed Mali in 2012, almost all remnants became allies of the Malian government by 2018. Some factions of movements such as the HCUA[22] and the MAA,[23] allies of the MLNA, are now part of the pro-Mali platform of participants in the Algiers Agreements of 2015 which ensconced peace between Mali and rebel movements and began integration processes under United Nations supervision.

Most notably, the MSA,[24] under the leadership of Mossa Ag Acharatoumane of the Dawsahak tribe, is very close with political leaders of the country. Mossa Ag Acharatoumane was one of the founding members of the MNLA. He was quite popular in 2012 with proponents of the Tamasheq insurgency. Born in 1986, highly dynamic and capable of debating and recruiting into the rationale of the rebellion, he was lauded as the future of

Azawad. His Facebook profile has been filled with enthusiastic comments and love declarations for years. He was one of the staunchest opponents of integration into Mali. Mossa Ag Acharatoumane embodied a glamourous vision of rebellion, seductive and indomitable when faced with antagonists during meetings, debates, or on television sets. Yet, nowadays, his ambitions are fully turned toward integration within Mali, and leadership in the application of the Algiers Agreements by his movement and his tribe whose natural leadership he has claimed for years even as elders were put aside in favor of his ability to obtain strength and cooperation from powerful allies such as French Opération Barkhane whose one-time leader General Bruno Guibert declared himself satisfied of cooperation between his cell and the MSA[25] as of July 2018. This was said amid grave allegations of human rights abuse by affiliates of the MSA in northeastern Mali and western Niger by various communities among whom local Fula.

For months, human rights organizations denounced the MSA as an actor of terror in that transborder areas, mostly with Fula communities as primary victims. The rationale of the MSA and Mossa Ag Acharatoumane told that they had been waging a just war against jihadists such as the Islamic State in the Greater Sahara (ISGS). The ISGS had allegedly been recruiting within Fula communities in priority. Hence, violence was a legitimate response in the narrative of the war of terror. Given the broad appeal of that narrative, it is no wonder that the MSA benefited from support both by France and its ally, the Malian government. In supporting the MSA as they have been doing, these parties have contributed to strengthen narratives of conspiracies against Fula people,[26] with the MSA being depicted as an opportunistic organization helping hegemonic agendas by the Dawsahak in the region, and letting them enjoy resources[27] that various communities usually compete over. It should be noted that this narrative depicting the MSA and the Dawsahak Tamasheq unfavorably has been used in other Tamasheq tribes and movements as well. All are vying for power and proximity with the powerful, at the cost of peace.

Tactical support and sharing of intelligence with Barkhane became perceived as an act of aggression against Fula people. Civil society leaders from Nigerien communities said as much during a meeting in August 2017[28] to discuss peace between Dawsahak and Fula. One source who was present at this meeting did a thorough work of transcribing feelings expressed by participants. Fula participants, by sharing their stories of victimization, settled on a general understanding that France, Mali, and Niger, with their allies of the G5 Sahel[29] Joint Force would be coming to destroy Fula societies and forever stain them with the false hypothesis of their collaboration with jihadists. Calls were made to assert Fula refusal of the G5 Sahel, as it appeared to be a menace to their local environment. With the alliance of G5 Sahel and the MSA, which is a legitimate group recognized by the international community since it is an offshoot of the MNLA and its wider organization, the Coordination of Movements of Azawad,[30] it subscribes to the terms of the Algiers Agreement—murders and pillaging plagued Fula communities as a result of the impunity in bands of Dawsahak fighters close to the MSA. In July 2018, a Fula child was heavily wounded during operations led by Barkhane. His recovery was paid for and publicized. Still, resentment did not abate, and neither did conviction that a grand plan was in motion against Fula people. The alliance between Barkhane and the MSA was not capable of maneuvering in a nuanced and open enough way so that the majority community throughout the Sahel, Fula, could feel included, listened to, and active in a grand narrative that could benefit them. In designing narratives about the war on terrorism, there has been some inability for creativity and thinking about new stories stemming from less vocal and martially powerful people. If the potential for cooperation with Fula groups was duly exploited, a major shift in the popular war on terrorism narrative might have been possible. In 2018, still, strategic planning, intelligence, and civilian-military cooperation had been unable to properly approach and unite all communities. Rather, it relied on dated tropes and dated narratives.

NOTES

1. De Bruijn et al., 2016.
2. A community of central Mali renowned for its specialization in fishing, and mobile activity on the River Niger.
3. Robinson, 1985.
4. Tabital Pulaaku is a global organization for the promotion of Fula cultures and the Fula language. Because of this, numerous members of the organization are not ethnically Fula. Most notably, communities where Fula tongues are spoken as vernacular languages, or that used to be under Fula domination, now embrace Tabital Pulaaku as an opportunity to cultivate a relationship with the part of their identity which stems from contact with Fula people.
5. Gina Dogon is a cultural organization, too. It deals mainly with the planning of cultural exhibitions and events, and promotion of Dogon heritage. Mostly since 2016, with the rise of interethnic clashes in the center of Mali and the heightened presence of jihadists, Gina Dogon has been called upon to help in mediation and peacebuilding. The organization is the primary interface for the media and for researchers seeking to earn introductions within Dogon communities.
6. Singular: *Kaaɗo*. This word derives from the Fula language radical meaning "that which is bitter/unseemly." Throughout the "Fula archipelago," the word "Kaaɗo" designates "Aliens," people who do not belong with Fula. Kaaɗo has been used as a general neutral ethnonym for Dogon, even in other languages, such as the majority Mande language Bamanankan. In our experience, it is deemed quite offensive to call a Dogon "Kaaɗo," most of all if one is known to have an understanding

of the meaning of the word and the stigma attached to it. Dogon were the neighboring "Haaɓe" of Fula in their homeland. Elsewhere, other peoples have been called Haaɓe. With the sway of jihadism in Dogon communities in the nineteenth century, non-Fula were expected to be less "civilized," being closer to olden religions. The sense of race that exists in Fula nation has also contributed to define what exactly it means to be a Kaaɗo. As one interlocutor took offense with us when we uttered the term "Haaɓe" in a conversation, it is important to indicate that even in non-tension contexts, with the fragility of the social fabric, "Kaaɗo" may trigger negative social memory. The gentleman who we had unfortunately offended explained that the term was deplorable because it meant, in his own word: *"Negroid, pagan sedentary people."* All these traits are features arguably contemptible according to general Fula standards. It remains to be determined to what extent Fula are less Negroid, less pagan, and less sedentary than their neighbors in all situations and contexts, though. That is precisely why it is important to take into account subjective experiences and to analyze them as valuable clues as to all the ways a topic should be handled with care.

7. Singular: *Ceddo*. This is another term that is used to indicate alienness. Again, depending on context, it may have different uses. In northern Senegal and southern Mauritania (the Fula homeland of Fuuta Tooro), for instance, Sebɓe are a caste of noblefolk with a concentration in martial traditions.

8. "Pour les Dogons et pour les chercheurs qui relaient leur point de vue, le *baji kan* est donc considéré comme le chant le plus immuable et le plus 'historique,' alors qu'il autorise la plus grande marge de création et d'improvisation" (Jolly, 2010).

9. Mouvement National de Mibération de l'Azawad (National Movement for the Liberation of Azawad, formerly known as MNA, National Movement of Azawad). Its initial name was "MNA," Mouvement National de l'Azawad (National Movement of Azawad) before they began violent actions.

10. "Accord D'Alger Pour La Restauration De La Paix, De La Sécurité Et Du Développement Dans La Région De Kidal | UN Peacemaker." United Nations. United Nations, July 4, 2006. https://peacemaker.un.org/mali-accordalger2006.

11. February 2015.

12. Azawad means "spoon" in Tamasheq languages. It corresponds to a hollow desert area in the north of Mali inhabited mainly by ethnic Tamasheq and ethnic Arabs. It is a topographic appellation first and foremost, and it was never a name for any polity in the north of Mali. The area spans Douentza Cercle in Mopti region and the three (at the time) regions of the north of Mali: Gao, Kidal, and Tombouctou. Though there were many Tamasheq polities in the north of Mali, they were centered on tribes and small- to medium-sized settlements, with no hegemonic expansive agenda. Thus, the use of Azawad by rebel groups starting in the 1990s was an attempt to create a narrative of unity among Tamasheq, to allow for more support for the cause, and, in unity, dismantle the state system which they rightfully blamed for their plights. Azawad is the name chosen by various Tamasheq rebel groups to refer to the area they view as the Tamasheq homeland. It became a consensual name. Historically, Tamasheq were never unified, though there were times of alliances between communities. Tamasheq are to be understood not as a monolithic people, but as an ensemble of peoples sharing languages and modes of correlating with one another. They do not have a single way of

60   Chapter 4

life or source of resources either. Depending on locations and lineages, some Tamasheq are herders, while others are scholars, or warriors, caravan traders, farmers, and so on.

13. The trauma of past crimes by the Malian army in the north of Mali, since at least 1963, is very much present in social memory and in psyches.

14. "A neighboring state."

15. From Swiss media *Le Temps*. Lema, L. (April 13, 2012). Le sanglot d'une Touareg du Mali. Retrieved from https://www.letemps.ch/monde/sanglot-dune-touareg-mali.

16. Guerre au Mali: Retour sur le drame d'Aguelhok—Jeune Afrique. (October 21, 2013). Retrieved from https://www.jeuneafrique.com/167687/politique/guerre-au-mali-retour-sur-le-drame-d-aguelhok/.

17. Five years after the massacre, Studio Tamani looks back at consequences of the attack. https://www.studiotamani.org/index.php/politique/10365-5-ans-apres-le-massacre-d-aguel-hoc-l-enquete-pietine.

18. From the 1970s, several Tamasheq families fled human rights abuses by governments of Mali intent on administering their lands with the same harshness and intransigence as colonial powers they succeeded upon the country's independence in 1960. Droughts in the 1970s and the 1980s also factored in, with inefficient assistance from the state. Libya became a safe haven where they found shelter and many youths joined elite forces of the Libyan army. Over several waves, from the 1980s to 2012, Tamasheq rebels were aided by their diaspora. The fall of Muammar Gaddafi with the international intervention of 2011 led by France caused political chaos in Libya and uncertainty for Tamasheq who were deemed too close to the fallen leader. As a result, highly trained Tamasheq fighters crossed over from the Libyan army into Tamasheq irredentist movements, and came to the aid of brethren in need in a destitute northern Mali in danger of being entirely toppled by violent Islamist movements. Alliances between the MNLA and jihadists was always going to be dangerous for the MNLA. They joined those they feared to fight enemies (the state), thinking they could broker a deal with jihadists to preserve their lands, not accounting for jihadist ideology of domination and dogmatic hegemony.

19. This is a list that was officially presented by the MNLA rebels themselves. Mnlamov. (January 27, 2013). Retrieved from http://malijet.com/actualite-politique-au-mali/flash-info/62837-le-mnla-devoile-la-liste-de-son-gouvernement.html.

20. This patronym is typical of Songhay people.

21. *Azashit*, in French. Also, online, we remember one commenter saying in 2012 that their university teacher had told them that Tamasheq arrived in North Africa from the Ruropean Balkans region, and that Arabs chased them off due to their being uncivilized, and this was how they'd arrived in Mali. This contradicts all scientific accounts proving that Tamasheq's ancestors, like other of other peoples of northern Mali, have be present for centuries (maybe Millennia).

22. High Council for the Unity of Azawad.

23. Arab Movement of Azawad.

24. Movement for the Salvation of Azawad.

25. Macé, C. (July 9, 2018). Au Sahel, "je n'ai pas besoin de canons supplémentaires, mais il nous faut gagner en mobilité." Retrieved from https://www.liberation

.fr/planete/2018/07/09/au-sahel-je-n-ai-pas-besoin-de-canons-supplementaires-mais-il-nous-faut-gagner-en-mobilite_1665186.

26. Niger: Des Peuls dénoncent les incursions et exactions d'ex-rebelles maliens. (May 7, 2018). Retrieved from https://www.rfi.fr/fr/afrique/20180507-niger-peuls-denoncent-incursions-exactions-milices-maliennes.

27. Wells, grazing areas, oases, and so on.

28. Meeting organized by French mediation organization *Promédiation*.

29. The G5 Sahel initiative is a comprehensive project for development and security in the Sahel. It was launched in December 2015 after a meeting organized in France between then French president François Hollande and leaders of Mauritania, Mali, Burkina Faso, Niger, and Chad. The G5 Sahel aims to realize lasting peace and security in the Sahel by supporting these five countries in development plans and joint military tasks. The Joint Force is the most sought-after project of the initiative. There is a clear tendency to reduce the G5 Sahel to this armed branch because security is presented as the primary challenge in the Sahel, and it is security measures that are being scrutinized and awaited with hope or fear.

30. Also, known as "The Coordination."

Chapter 5

Looking toward Lasting Paradigms

"FULANESS" AND PULAAKU

With so much talk about Fula peoples and their links with jihadism, little analysis exists on the factors that put them at risk in violent contexts and how narratives about their plights have been produced over the ages. These narratives are employed for peacebuilding, or warmongering, depending on ideologies regarding the future of Fula people. There is a constant rhetorical discourse about actions globally connected Fula should take to protect themselves. Within Fula communities themselves, the conclusion that Fula are being victimized in all their homelands slowly prevailed. This became a normal sentiment. Fula being heterogeneous community native to some twenty African countries, anyone would be hard-pressed to assert any general trend. Rather, those audible communities and opinion leaders in Fula communities are those one may rely on for analysis. Because of high heterogeneity and numbers, it is nigh-impossible to know with exactitude how many Fula exist. Additional factors in determining who is a Fula arise because of the high diversity in community lifestyles,[1] too. Fula are believed to be the "people of the cow" because of the high esteem they show toward cattle herding and the possession of cows, most specifically. Even when they do not possess cattle, Fula will remind others of their attachment to cows and herding, as a continual remembrance of their true nature as ancient herders. Likewise, nomadism is considered a staple of Fula identity. However, nowadays, most Fula are settled in sedentary communities. Islam is closely linked to Fula identity now, but that was not always the case. Some Fula are considered to be closer to the old ways. They have a very mild practice of Islam, and they are mostly rural Fula. Fula were champions of Islamic proselytism and the spread of Islam in Africa (most notably in the nineteenth century), jihadism is recalled in conversations involving Fula identity of violent events related to Fula. The Fula language itself should not be considered as an inalienable component of Fula identity, for many a Fula person or community does not speak any Fula tongue. Some even proudly clamor their distance with the language of their ancestors.[2]

In our experience with Fula across Africa and in the diaspora,[3] the one element that is nigh universal in all Fula communities is the acknowledgment of some code of ethics deemed to be proper to Fula people. This code is usually called "Pulaaku,"[4] the way of being a Fula, though it may even not be named. It is knowledge of being different as a people and knowing codes of ethics deemed as different from those of outgroups. Components of Pulaaku may vary, but the main tenets are universal throughout the Fula archipelago. *Hersa* comes first. Then, there are *munyal*, *gacce*, and *hakkilo*. *Hersa* means shame, as in knowing the sense of shame and modesty. It is a stepping stone of stereotypical interactions involving Fula, and it comes as a posterior explainer of interactions with Fula, to justify their physical distance with others, their meekness, and their overall aloofness. *Munyal* is endurance in the face of adversity, and generally any struggle: lust, hunger, pain, and so on. *Gacce* is the respect for others' space and their dignity. It is about preserving others' integrity and not overly asserting or imposing oneself. *Hakkilo* is general good sense and wisdom. These codes of ethics are interpreted as necessary trials to foster within oneself, regardless of gender, in order to survive well as a Fula, among visibly different communities,[5] and out in the wilderness, traveling or herding, since nomadism and herding are still considered to be vestiges of the birth of Fula identity, in popular Fula narratives. There is a great deal of performativity in Pulaaku and its display, with varying modes of operation depending on the audience: Fula or not, African or not.

Pulaaku, as "the way of being a Fula" and the set of rules of ethics transmitted in Fula communities across Africa, may be summoned in Fula narratives about conflict. We have observed that in any given Fula community gathering, references are made to how behavior should be applied in order to remain noble and to withhold Pulaaku. Conversely, Pulaaku, while praised, is paradoxically blamed as one of the reasons why Fula are victimized. "It is because we know shame and we will not sully ourselves that we are being held back," as we have heard so often.

FULA IDENTITY DYNAMICS AND THE VALUE OF A TRANSNATIONAL APPROACH

Delafosse (1912) explains how national and ethnic narratives must be taken carefully, given their continued shaping after Fula's introduction of Islam in their regions. He points out the subtle ways through which genealogies and claims have been aligned to fit into episodes of Islamization and the birth and rise of Islam. Legendary ancestors are made to descend from Islamic heroic figures.

Fula people have long narrated themselves as a community of people living across Africa, with roots in ancient countries of yore in a mythical Africa. When we started interviewing Fula people for the purpose of various university dissertations,[6] between 2008 and 2010, we found that many youths (our subject pool was comprised of people of different genders, between ages twenty-one and twenty-six, of African Fula descent, and living in Europe) viewed the land of "origins" of their ancestors as Ethiopia, or Ancient Egypt, or a promised faraway land whose name had been forgotten. Fula identity, in self-assertions, is more often than not tied with the idea of being foreign and coming from distant lands, with narratives rooted in herding and the nomadic nature of Fula people. Difference from other communities creates the primary marker for how identity is defined. This may be summarized as such: "I am not you, and that is why I am myself." Throughout our various experiences, we have heard Fula people explain how Pulaaku made them different, how their sophisticated transnational (and transcontinental[7] even) ancestry meant they were not racially like any other peoples of Africa, how Fula had ruled nations, and so on. And nowadays, even with divisions in Fula societies, there is an attempt at essentializing Fula identity around codified and set standards such as race and culture.[8] Slogans such as the now-famous "Lenyol Gootol, Demngal Gootal"[9] are abundant. Modern modes of communication enable and facilitate these processes. Fula people have a consciousness of themselves being different and that they possess their very own history and narratives about themselves, even as each community will pride itself in its worth and its originality. This contributes to the feeling of solidarity among Fula people and to the great attention with which Fula people observe incidents that involve their kinsfolks from other regions and countries. "It could be us," they say. Many Fula organizations have "Panfula" ambitions, aiming to federate global Fula civil society initiatives. The most famed and accepted organization is "Tabital Pulaaku," "Promoting Fula Culture."

Tabital Pulaaku is oftentimes accused of being one of the catalysts of brazen Fula identity self-expression.[10] As a community organization, it is identified first and foremost as a biased defender of the communities it seeks to advocate for. Thus, instead of being accepted as a legitimate actor of mediation, interposition, and pedagogy, community organizations are attacked as proponents of division.[11] But is division inherent to diversity? Problems in Mali massively rely on the difficulty to be united while accepting difference. This is a universal debate in times of globalization and fear of subjugation. Individual identities, fearing their disappearance, must weigh the benefits and the costs of subscribing to broader all-encompassing movements, such as nation-states. This makes the position of community organizations very delicate. They do not wish to betray the ideals they promote within their communities. Concomitantly, they do not want to be depicted as separatists, since they may acknowledge the dangers of divisionism, and also see the harsh consequences of going rogue as rebel organizations have. The balance to keep is tenuous between assertiveness and aggression. The ability to successfully push for an agenda relies quite a lot on the leeway allowed by states.

In Mali, defending a community in the post-traumatic context of the rebellion of 2012 has been straining. In 2013, after the initial success of the French intervention with Opération Serval, a roadmap for reconstruction was discussed before the parliament. During one of the sessions, then representative of Douentza,[12] Fatoumata Dicko, upon firmly expressing her worry that Malian troops were violating human rights and killing civilians as they moved forward in their land operations, was heckled by a majority of her colleagues. She was obliged to return to her seat, with only little support from some other colleagues. Attempts to defend communities of origin, or to criticize the narrative of war on terror and absolute supremacy of righteous Grand Mali were met with great repulsion. This would, in time, prove to have been a grave mistake, as that time in the history of Mali held many clues as to what would unfold in the future, about the level of vulnerability of the center of the country. These clues and elements on central Mali's vulnerability were strengthened by rampant victimization of Fula people in Mali and in neighboring countries.

It is essential to analyze Fula identity politics through an understanding of Fula as a transnational community and a nation of interwoven stories and relationships. As such, we cannot discount Malian Fula social memory and narratives from other countries as they contribute to an overall pool of "Fulaness" that is both acknowledged and shared by Fula communities. In the age of information, the *Fula archipelago*'s already porous transnational borders are made less and less clear. Information Technology has become the immaterial transhumance road connecting all Fula. Fula communities have always entertained kinship and proximity with each other, even across wide swaths of land, and despite geography, hence the idea of a Fula archipelago for a Fula nation. Globalization is not new for Fula people, and its modern tools are providing great opportunities for jointly shaping ideas of Fula identity. It is, thus, absolutely essential to not negate the effects of seemingly outside influences in Mali's Fula issues. This may be true for other communities, too, be they nomadic and transnational, or not.[13]

One major narrative used by Fula in times of conflict is that of them being victims of a plot by other communities in order to eradicate them. Sad figures of Fula around Africa being targeted in farmers versus herders conflicts are omnipresent in news articles and over social media. Every time major clashes occur and gory pictures circulate, it is as if there happens an awakening of past traumas. In family circles and discussion groups on Facebook, WhatsApp, and so on, outcries and calls for vengeance are mingled with self-admonishment about the failure to act. During our past research on Fula identity,[14] we had interviewed individuals from several West African countries about what it meant for them to be Fula. In their narrations of their family lines, they often painted trails made of vivid social memories of struggle, migration, and near-destruction: "My ancestors fled barbarism in Macina," "We were lucky to find a homeland where we could settle for good," "Because others do not like us, we had to stick with each other." In recent history, several Fula communities have been at risk. In Guinea, the regime of Sékou Touré, the first president of the country, acted out executions and discrimination against Fula, based on the belief that they were internal agents of Western imperialistic powers aiming to depose his regime and take over.[15] This was based on stereotypes of Fula as being shrewd, racist, and incapable of accepting domination by "Black" people they deemed to be inferior to them. Indeed, the narrative of Fula as endogamic and racist exists both within and without their community. There is, indeed, a certain high regard for racial purity. As much as *Fulaness* is based on the knowledge and application of Pulaaku, descent and racial conformity are greatly expected, too, and this even in spite of the incredible phenotypical diversity of Fula. The classical type expected of Fula has been well described throughout history, with fascination by Europeans fueling standardizations of what it means to be physically Fula. This was the times of colonization, physical anthropology, and scientific racism. Fula, upon being encountered by Westerners, were described as remnants of Indo-European invaders.[16] French explorers, most notably, were awestruck by the physique of Fula and were quick to want to classify them in the category of "Hamites," "races" deemed to be intermediate between "Indo-Europeans" and "Negroes." Truthfully, Fula come in all shades and shapes, though the more "negroid" kind is oftentimes deemed to be less "pure." We believe that there is still no way to scientifically assert such a thing. As long as all individuals within the great spectrum of *Fulaness* continue to identify as Fula, we cannot assert who is pure or not. Still, in minds, in subjectivity, pure-blooded *real* Fula are those individuals who display classical narrated Fula physical archetypes with copper-hued skin, soft curly hair to straight hair, aquiline and stretched noses, thin bone structure and a slender build, almond eyes, and an overall sense of beauty, dignity, and delicacy. Fula people believe themselves to be the offspring from the mixing of an ancient light-skinned people come from the east with darker-skinned Africans.

The number of strong political entities created or led by Fula made them a force to be reckoned with and a people admired and feared, instilling in future generations of Fula a sense that they come from a great, intelligent, and beautiful people whose heritage needs to be staunchly defended, even as Fula very often know little about the life conditions of Fula lifestyles very different from theirs, such as is the case for settled Fula versus nomads, or Fula from the Sahel versus Fula from southern reaches of western and central Africa.

The idea that Fula view themselves as better than others has been used to preemptively attack them. It has been used by Fula as well to take distance from danger and to intellectually reinforce the need to "take the higher road." This narrative of Fula aloof dignity has been criticized today within Fula communities. As we read it on an Internet page: "Fula are the most blessed nation in the world, with the worst strategies ever"—meaning that Fula stances about violence made them particularly vulnerable to attacks. These words echo declarations on WhatsApp groups or during casual conversations uttered in lament. They are said in reference not only to warmongering but also solidarity, poverty, development, cultural projects, and so on.

Fear of total eradication is constant in Fula calls for action. This narrative of "Haaɓe" or "Baleeɓe"[17] threatening to destroy Fula completely is summoned to rile up masses and gain favor and support, both morally and financially. In December 2013, probably because we are a researcher and social activist of Fula persuasion,[18] we received in our personal physical mailbox (in France) a pamphlet titled "Alerte sur la préparation du génocide contre les Peuls et le projet de guerre civile en Moyenne Guinée."[19] This document was widely circulated over the Internet and sent to prominent Fula individuals, human rights organizations, international organizations, and the Western media. The intent of the authors was to blow the whistle on the racialization of politics in Guinea, and the danger Fula were allegedly being put in by populist tactics of President Alpha Condé and his government. They provided insight on past victimization of Fula during the times of Sékou Touré, and during the political transition in 2009,[20] during the elections of 2010,[21] and on narratives being served to foster conflict and hold power. The tone of the pamphlet seemed overly empathetic. Contacts who received the document later told us that they, too, felt the tone was overly empathetic and many times inappropriate. They failed to see how the document could be taken seriously, or as something other than a political attempt to sabotage the regime of President Alpha Condé, using sensationalism. In other words, the mixing of facts with *ad hominem* attacks, and a very offensive writing style, displayed the features of a narrative that was immediately identified as skewed and dangerous. The document has remained on the Internet, and it has been feeding the immaterial object that is Fula identity, creating some more fuel to the weaponization of Fula victimhood in order to gain favors from the diaspora and outside observers at a global level.

Observation from the international community has been ambiguous. Colonial fantasies played a major role in Fula identity dynamics after contacts with Europeans. Racial defense of Fula and racial attack of them are both seeped with narratives born in the Western world. In their attempts to rationalize Fula glory and physical types, Western scientists tried to find correspondences between Fula and various people from outside West Africa. Besides the mythical so-called Indo-Europeans riders whose progeny is said to be all these Hamites who were newly created, more exotic examples existed,[22] among which Dravidians, Ethiopians, Ancient Egyptians, and even survivors of the doom in Atlantis, or "redskin Indians." Hebrews were certainty among the most popular hypothetical kinsfolk of Fula, both as per Westerners as per Fula themselves. Romantic notions and stereotypes about wandering and nomadism, high intelligence, miscegenation and ancient racial mixing, racial anthropology, fueled approximations between Fula tales and Hebraic lore. During the times of Sékou Touré, Fula social memory was marked by vitriolic speeches about Fula being parasites, bastards, stateless traitors. Just as we previously indicated, influences of violence and barbarism in the colonial army being transmitted into local African armies at the onset of African independences should be recalled, too. This is speculation in our part and it should be tested and researched in different works. Internalized racism and antisemitism may have carried over into the mental repertoires of Africans who came in close contact with Europe. There is most likely ground for discussing the mark of European antisemitism in racist narratives in postcolonial Africa. But just as antisemitism was used to harm Fula, so have Fula themselves reappropriated discourses equating their fate to that of Jews. This was not only through complaint. The stereotypical famed and lauded Jewish mind and ability for travel and integration (while keeping a sense of identity) where reappropriated, too, as well as militant stances about isolationism and separation as a reaction to barbarism. As a case in point, on Jamaa, Tabital Pulaaku's defunct listserv, there were several discussions about these issues, with very polarized views. Though Jamaa ultimately opened up to many different contributors, it was initially a media involving Fula elites, decision makers, journalists, and other influential types. Because of this particular nature, it is both a location for the dissemination of information and for advocacy. Hence, many try to appeal to Fula communities through Jamaa, though it also served as a platform for scientific discussions,[23] community announcements, and so on. In 2014, during a discussion on human rights advocacy in Fula communities, a contributor claimed that they discouraged their relatives in attempts to mingle with "Blacks," they insisted that Fula, "like Berber," were stuck between "plague (Blacks)" and "cholera (Arabs)." They called for the end of ethnic mixing and for separation from other ethnicities who they viewed as "barbaric." There was a consensus in responses, with outcry and consternation being the overwhelming reactions. No contributor was found to publicly espouse the views defended by this person. Some voiced very tame attempts to mitigate. But these were mainly non-visible contributors.[24] Side-talks suggested that this was the work of a "troll"[25] either trying to push for an extremist Fula agenda of their own or seeking to goad public figures into speaking in inappropriate manners. One organization leader, T.B., told us they believed this was a way of speaking that "no Fula could express it, it is such a blatant caricature of Fula extremism that it must be the work of an outsider." It seemed important for T.B. to express that this could not be the "work" of someone caring about Fula and how they are perceived in their native environments. Since these days, Jamaa has lost much of its popularity, in part because of censorship after more and more voices began to express polarized reactions after Fula victimization was reported more and more frequently. Jamaa could no longer contain outrage, nor did it suffice to express nonconventional ideas. Mainly, relatedly, the advent of WhatsApp and other more participative platforms was the dirge of the unified space that was Jamaa. Now, conversations are taken to Facebook pages and groups, regardless of their editorial content. Whether on *Fulanitube*, *Zone Fulbe*, or *Communauté Peule*, complaints and cries about Fula victimization are told with little restraint, though different moderation policies affect the future of these messages once they are posted.

In 2016, as Fula organizations were holding a World Congress of Pulaaku in Burkina Faso, Facebook posts from Guinea and Mali denounced an attempt by Fula elites (namely Ali Nouhoum Diallo[26] and Cellou Dalein Diallo[27]) to proclaim the birth of a new Fula state.

Within the atmosphere of heightened rivalry between Fula and Maninka in Guinea, ethnic tensions have been steadily rising since the times of the country's independence (in 1958), and more particularly since 2009. The rise of Sekou Touré, the country's first president, and the opening of political power to Fula elites of Guinea in 2009 have reinvigorated ancient rivalries—albeit at different times—and put in danger elements of national cohesion. This idea concerns Mali too, as it has been deemed to be with Guinea "two lungs within one shared body." Mali and Guinea have very different realities, so where do their commonalities rest? Surely at least in great part on Mande and its legacy. The case of social tension in Guinea is just one among various cases in which Fula victimization is observed throughout the Fula diaspora. The war in the Central African Republic, Burkina Faso's very own war on terror, everyday conflicts between farmers and herders, have all been providing tragic traumatic content that has been affecting Fula people's visions of themselves as a single suffering people. The same diaspora members who feel great sorrow about these situations have been sending thoughts and resources to Fula people around the world, to foster efforts of help in the field. Violent support was also discussed on various platforms, with the security crisis in Mali. Fula of different parts of Africa have been expressing a desire to help self-defense groups in the field and to get them weapons, ammunition, and public relations support in the Western world. As such, for peacebuilding, Fula diasporas and their influence cannot be ignored. Attempts to ridicule and show scorn for the meddling of "foreigners" into internal state affairs[28] has not been productive. If anything, we have noticed that this prickles the sense of Fula's common identity. Approaches based on inclusion of diaspora actors as a factor for conciliation may be more useful.

One additional narrative complementing "the curse of Fula," and the "conspiracy for Fula genocide" (as well as the external and internal narrative of "Fula elitism") is that of "the rebirth of the Fula nation." The idea goes that after so much hardship and so much meekness, Fula must finally get together and fight back. It is not so much about fighting as it is about fighting back. It is entertaining for many to think of this as "Make Fula Great Again" since an important part of this idea rests on the thought that Fula dominated in an indefinite romanticized narrated past. There is also a notion, often backed by colonial tales and their contemporary analyses, that Fula hegemony was broken by colonial penetration. Hence, vying for a Fula identity and domination revival would be setting Fula back on the trails they had been destined for. However, there was no united plan for Fula domination even at the peak of the century, which truly was the golden age of Fula conquests, the nineteenth century. The very idea of a unified Fula nation is a modern notion. That does not negate the existence of a shared sense of belonging. Looking at Fula as a monolithic entity is certainly a mistake, though, and a dangerous one at that. In 2016, a report indicated that "Nigerian Fulani Militants" were the fourth most murderous terrorist group in the world.[29] The report went on to be relayed by various media, disseminating a narrative about "Fula revolt" which unfortunately does correlate with the internal "Fula survival" narrative in their featuring the idea of a surge in Fula identity politics. The situation in Nigeria is very different from that of Mali. We do see a familiar danger in communication about mass violence in Nigeria, though. Fula are not a united group and several bands act of their own accord. Actions are not coordinated. There is a context of civil war in those states where Fula bands are attacking civilians, making reporting crimes they are committing as simple terrorism a strange description, however atrocious and massive they may be. Such articles have been widely discussed in Fula groups around the world, with a sense of anger about depictions of Fula, creating resentment about what was interpreted as partiality against Fula people, once more. In Nigeria, Taraba State, Plateau State, and Adamawa State have very different contexts of apparition for these militant groups. However, their issues are conflated, and all Fula tend to be shoehorned into the conflict, starting with President

Muhammadu Buhari himself, who is of Fula ancestry. President Buhari,[30] a Fula himself, is accused of letting Fula herders kill "indigenous people" because they are his kin, and he is allegedly trying to support their agendas. This, very much like tactics of pushing into meekness and shaming Fula leaders, silences them. These tactics prove very useful in disabling Fula defense against violence. With a simplified narrative of Fula as savage "allogeneic" invaders, it becomes easier to justify crackdowns. Identity and motives of opposing parties are blended together to serve a greater narrative that would allow less control and transparency over operations, be it for populist reasons, financial reasons, or moral reasons. These conflations resonate with dangerous narratives seeking to turn Fula into heroes of fundamental armed Islam. This, too, taps into manipulation of historical facts with a skewed contemporary perspective. Since Fula have held realms that conveyed Islam, imposed it, and ruled under its tenets, and since their fervor was acknowledged in written and well-documented accounts, mass access to knowledge helps simplifying the shape of past reality. Fula, even as they spread Islam aggressively were, once again, never united behind one brand of Islam or one political vision. That is precisely why Fula theocratic states fell, as they became rivals or were not able to enlist help from neighbors or brethren. Identity was not a factor of success or cohesion, then. It was simply a reality that created bonds, without superimposing political ventures among groups.

OF JIHADISTS AND DOZO

Since the MUJWA's time in Douentza, the term "jihadist" has become an all-encompassing term to designate problematic Fula groups in Mali. Even as dubious Fula self-defense movements were quick to advertise that they are not fighting for religious ideals but for protection and survival, there has always been doubt about the sources of the support they got in terms of weapons and training. Trending idea that posited that jihadism was trying to become indigenous throughout Africa and the Sahel, encouraging public perceptions of certain communities as being targeted by Jihadists for recruitment and being closer to them. With the history of many Fula communities as past champions of Islam, it has become generally accepted that Fula people are highly Islamized and still feel close to jihadism since jihadism was a primary factor in the settlement of Fula people in present-day countries. A high-ranking government official we spoke with in Mali in March 2018 told us that Fulfulde, the Fula language, was the primary language of jihadist recruitment and that jihadists were relying on feelings of loyalty to historical jihads, in order to penetrate Fula societies and enroll Fula. It is a narrative built from stereotypes about Fula people. The majority of Fula people in areas where jihadists hold sway in Mali have always heavily relied on pastoralism. They do not hail from clerical castes of Fula societies, though they often have blood connections to them. As a result of this, there was interest in shifting power balances. Jihadist movements most certainly benefited from the idea that they are close to Fula people, as that helps to polarize communities. It similarly helps them legitimize their position as defenders of Fula communities and natural allies of them. Even with the lack of evidence for mass recruitment, and as the number of jihadists in the center of Mali never seemed to go above figures of a few hundreds, the idea of the jihadist peril upon Macina and the world through the hands of Fula people continued to propagate, damaging perceptions of Fula civilians and fostering very real attempts of mass revolt by Fula groups facing arrests, murders, and intimidation by neighboring communities and agents of the state fueled by fear, revenge, or instrumentalization, in order to seize resources belonging to Fula people. Many groups that are labeled as jihadists are Fula militias. That does not make them any less violent or dead. But it does give a different view on their strategies and endgames.

It is not only outsiders who call these groups jihadists, though. Presenting oneself as being jihadist-adjacent as an immediate effect of tapping into terrorism's strength in instilling fear, and making oneself appear more menacing. Ultimately, it does not seem this is very useful since the spiral of fear and anxiety leads to more polarization and violence.

Similarly, what is called "Dozo" truly refers to a brotherhood of hunters of Mande origins[31] with esoteric knowledge of plants and animals. They traditionally hold initiation rites that are necessary for them to accept new members, after years of training. However, through the media and through a deliberate strategy to gain legitimacy by insurgent groups of the center of Mali, militias introduced themselves as Dozo, or supported gray areas thanks to the manipulation of which they could sell the narrative of themselves as defenders of the land and the people, and opponents of anti-state jihadists. Civilians from the center of Mali were silent or silenced because of the fear of reprisals by armed groups (militias, jihadists, Dozo) or the possibility that if all armed groups disappear, they would indeed be left to fend for themselves. And so, traditional hunters could appear as a necessary evil in some farming communities, just as jihadists may for Fula people. Little care is given to the fact that not everyone can up and join Dozo groups. It is after a long secret process that males may become Dozo.[32] Thus, the appearance and the numbers of Dozo in the center of Mali is certainly misleading.

Even though in neighboring countries like Côte D'Ivoire,[33] there has been a gradual rise of Dozo militias disconnected from tradition, as defenders of civilians in times of unrest, it can hardly be said that "real" Dozo—even when they have indeed gone through the formal process of enrollment as proper

Dozo—do benefit from a mandate by civilians to represent them. Therein lies a great difficulty of approaches that would make Dozo natural responses to jihadism and intercommunity violence. Dozo do not have a monolithic top-down way of functioning with a democratic base delineating their mandates and missions. It has been gradually difficult to ascertain precisely who the so-called Dozo of the center of Mali, with their sometimes foreign cars, really have been, and whether their agendas were based on territory, racism, or anti-jihadism. What is certain is that they have left destruction, hate speech, and acts of ethnic cleansing in the wake of their dominions in parts of central Mali. Entire villages were burned down, entire clans were evicted because of the presence of these militias dressed as revered hunters. The future would prove how deadly these militias were.

"Fake jihadists" and "fake Dozo" create tension and polarization around identities. They contribute to affirmations of hostility rooted in identity narratives, in order to find ways to protect one's community. Social memory is summoned to remind that Fula people have been jihadists for centuries, or to say that Fula people's neighbors hate them and would ally with any foreign groups to kick them out. "Real" jihadists certainly benefit from such tensions as they weaken social resilience to their actions and prove how weak the Malian government had been from 2012 to 2018, and how necessary a new purification of mores had been necessary in order to bring about Islamic peace and harmony, albeit with great violence.

Those groups facilitating hunters' actions still have unclear agendas. One may hypothesize, though, that weapon circulation in Mali represents a tremendous opportunity to gain money. The murkiness of governance in Mali has allowed organized crime to thrive, as well. As such, jihadists or criminals benefit from chaos, as they can not only become more present but also use that presence and their alliances to exploit vulnerable peoples further. With self-righteous narratives of social-political just, they have deviated popular needs to extend hegemonic violent rules.

With this picture, we must insist that being categorical and setting paradigms based on macro-groups is of very little use in the understanding of violence in Mali, as allegiances and narratives are quite often untied from real-life everyday activities and allegiances of civilians. Pragmatic circumstances overrule paradigms. Still, the "souls" of civilians and the legitimacy to speak in their names has become a commodity that allows armed groups to expand power.

IN SEARCH OF PROTAGONISTS?

History is surely in the making in Mali, in times of strife and destruction. Human beings were attacked. Communities were attacked. Symbols were attacked as narratives have been undone either by deliberate words or by breaking their grandiosity and positive components, such as Mali's invulnerability being undone by war defeat. For Malian Fula, the crossroads of 2012–2018 was decisive in shaping social memory. Some years later, it seems that there are no more heroes. Doesn't every story deserve a hero? One would be hard-pressed to find Fula figures ascending into the pantheon of future Malian Fula narratives. Elites from Fula communities have been harshly criticized throughout both in-group and outgroup discussions about Fula's situation in Mali. They have been depicted as glib and corrupt leaders who are uninterested in the future of citizens they allegedly view as plebes. Some depict them as warmongers intent on secretly developing Fula supremacist agendas, or powerless bystanders who need to be replaced. These rather negative images certainly stem from racist narratives, when coming from outside of the community. Racism does not fully account for such hostile depictions, though. As we have demonstrated earlier in this work, pressure for national integration in Mali makes community-centered advocacy extremely fraught with suspicions of sabotaging the national fabric. As such, community elites and advocates often fear that their intents may be distorted to feed into reactions based on the national dogma of "One diverse nation-state of Mali with no exceptional peoples, but one exceptional people." In that view, Mali ambivalently prides itself in its diversity, all the while denying possibilities of stressing issues that are particular to one alternate identity. Mali has diversity, but it does not experience pluralism[34] in political claims. Our own experience briefly working for the Malian delegation at the UNESCO[35] made this apparent. Topics related to indigenous rights[36] were not retained as they did not appear to serve a greater national purpose yet. Thus, singular identities were destined for integration to state volition and not grassroots aspirations. One Malian diplomat (not working at the delegation, then) confided and expressed that leaders of Malian diplomacy were constantly wary of displeasing political leaders of Mali, when, at the same time, most of the public opinion of Mali was quite opposed to too visible forms of identity and minority claims. Rebellions by Tamasheq in Mali instilled the idea that any identity and minority claim was a potential danger to the existence of Mali and to the Malian narrative of unity. Marginal voices were dangerous voices, even if they came from communities as numerous in Mali as Fula. With that scope of analysis, it is easier to see how Fula elites may feel daunted and challenged at several levels when advocating on the basis of their identity. From within Fula communities, power plays between strata of each of Fula societies create a situation of competition for power with elites. Differences in allegiances toward the state also factor in the questioning of Fula elites. The very fact that elites would feel intimidated by outside influences (by the state, the public opinion at large) ensured that they would feel inhibited. That inhibition in taking action proves to be the source of criticism by Fula masses for whom, then, elites seem to be only interested in preserving a stalemate that would preserve their privileges within the state of Mali.

Specific figures of the so-called Fula elite have been dealing with criticism throughout the crisis. Among them, three cases may help paint a comprehensive picture of how the molding of sustainable and strengthening narratives has not been working. Communities and their members' involvement in peacebuilding rest on symbols and feelings of hope outpouring from positive figures and narratives. Thus, visible protagonists represent elements of strength or weakness. In considering some major Fula protagonists of the Malian crisis, we will be looking at different ways in which the emergence of positive Fula figures is challenged. That certainly contributes to damaging internal regulation levers and feelings of being secure within Fula communities. Without these elements, to what extent is it possible to earn community involvement? Without heroes, how can there be peace? How do we find repercussions of these narratives on personal actions and agency? An approach based on individuals may offer some insight on topics of gender, caste, or interpersonal relations, which are not always visible in the bigger picture, but do matter in conflict comprehension. Such an approach would necessitate longitudinal studies, in addition to this monographic work.

Looking at the gender of protagonists, women in Fula politics are active, but they are usually invisible in leadership positions. When they are, they are deputized under male leadership. Hence, it is important that we cite the interesting case of Fatoumata Dicko, a former representative[37] of Douentza (Mopti region, central Mali) at the national parliament of Mali. Dicko has been a deputy vice president of the Malian chapter of Tabital Pulaaku. Moreover, she also hails from the royal family of Dallah (Douentza Cercle). She has held political functions, has been an activist, and she benefits from traditional sway. One could argue that this concentration of powers should make it easier to advocate. Yet, when she protested human rights abuses by the Malian army in 2013 before her fellow representatives, she was met with harsh rebuttals and accusations of weakening morale and sullying the name of the Republican Institution that are the FAMA.[38] During several discussions and collaborations between 2015 and 2018, she provided us with information about the daily plights of Fula from central Mali and all communities in general, with some focus on children and women. Namely, she described various cases she had been called to solve: widows seeking justice after attacks by soldiers or militias, teenagers who had been detained by the army as they were suspected of being jihadists, herding women who were denied exit from their settlements by jihadists as they wanted to bring their cattle to grazing areas, and so on. Gender issues were one topic among others she got knowledge of thanks to her deep roots in Fula communities as a woman. As a woman, she did not engage specifically on women's issues, though. Advocating, she would recall the various hardships met by civilians. She certainly possessed specific gender expertise men had not. As of the time of this work, women's leadership in Fula communities had not risen, though. With the immensity of problems, community-centered approaches have tended to concentrate on general advocacy, rather than gender advocacy. Community being a more visibly root variable in the origin of conflicts than gender is, it creates more interest. Gender, then, becomes a subsection of community-based violence. In the Malian crisis, women's depictions aimed to garner sympathy, by their description as victims, pillars of social life, who needed to be saved. Fula women themselves are the subject of stereotypes and stigma that are specific to them. There is intersectionality between their identity as Fula and their identity as women. Fula women are seen as seductive and deceitful. This makes the question of gender in interactions with Fula quite sensitive to comprehend. After an investigation led by members of our human rights organization, Kisal, in neighboring northern Burkina Faso, one of our female colleagues called us to discuss the question of gender-based violence (GBV), most especially gender-based sexual violence. This should be analyzed with consideration regarding all its components. This is violence that involves sex and sexual body parts, and which women are subjected to because of their status and identity as women (differently from other genders). Our colleague went on to explain that the number of Fula women who had been victims of such violence was highly underestimated. A case in point was the harrowing story that had just been confided to her by a relative from the countryside: several women had allegedly been raped by Burkinabe soldiers. But no one told. And no one would tell. The sense of shame was too great. No man could be told. No *Kaado* could be told. Fula women would have had to engage with these women and build trust in order to hear about such violations. And so, these violations would not come up in most news reports. Mentions of them could be minimized, with no systematic ways of verifying them, as false narratives meant to confuse or earn sympathy. This is unfortunate since Fula women might be confidantes for their sisters, but also investigators, champions, advocates, officials. That would, however, come with tremendous stress and continuous challenges both from within their communities (in systemic misogyny) and outside of out (by manipulated negative stereotypes of Fula women into silencing them). Additionally, they would have to hold leadership all the while owning up and displaying their identity as Fula women in countries that would deny ethnicity on political stages, with fears of encouraging tribalism and identity politics. This is true in Burkina Faso, as it is true in Mali. Though we have encountered Fula women in leading positions, such as Fatoumata Dicko, or Kadiatou Sow,[39] oftentimes advocating for Fula human rights and for Fula women's living conditions, they are not publicly regarded as figures that are absolute unavoidable figures when it comes to Fula issues, thought they do the work. They are deputized, while men are assumed to be more competent in leadership.

Ali Nouhoum Diallo, a native of Douentza Cercle, is a physician by trade. He was one of the founding members of ADEMA-PASJ, and he was the president of Mali's single chamber parliament for two terms, from 1992 to 2002. He later went on to also lead the ECOWAS'[40] parliament. Hailing from a family of the common nobility,[41] he is often depicted as a man of great personal humility. Diallo describes himself as the son of two illiterate Fula herders.[42] When the MUJWA took control of Douentza in 2012, they chiefly tried to recruit in destitute herding communities, as opposed to the politically powerful traditional ruling families (such as the related Dicko royal lineages of Boni and Dallah).[43] The struggles of Fula herders vying for more control over pastures[44] had led to a feeling of division between traditional elites and commoners of all castes. Most particularly, herders, being highly dependent on transhumance corridors and safe passage were made vulnerable because of the physical insecurity created during the MNLA's rebellion. This added up to feelings of frustration caused by poor governance and unequal access to resources that were very much founded on traditional cronyism, financial power, and political commerce. Though local Fula aristocrats are proud descendants of herders, they do not rely on pastoralism as a principal source of livelihood and finances. With no support during the occupation by the MNLA, herders did not find advocates. As the MUJWA rose in power, they were under an alien religious rule which they were not accustomed to, for it brought on a rigorist form of Islam unlike their more tolerant kind. The MUJWA did bring a sense of justice and fairness as it threatened failing elites and flogged thieves and wrongdoers. While it cannot be said that locals supported the MUJWA, they did find norms and regulations that were reliable, unlike the chaos of the previous months and the injustice they had been subjected to even before 2012. When the Malian army conquered back Douentza Cercle in early 2013, mass arrests occurred in herding communities. Herders were accused of having allied with the MUJWA, of being informants, or downright jihadists. This led to defiance against government actions. Ali Nouhoum Diallo, throughout the occupation of Douentza, has advocated for more justice and understanding of the precariousness of herders' situations. Because of this, he has been called an apologist of jihadism. As Diallo criticized the inefficiency in governance in Mali and the crimes committed by Malian soldiers, he was depicted as a brazen racist, with imagery that taps into well-known anxieties about Fula hegemony. On social media, some opponents called Diallo "the most racist man in Mali," an "advocate of separatism in Mali." At least two soldiers we have spoken with between 2012 and 2018 said that trouble in central Mali would end "if Ali Nouhoum Diallo and Général Ismaïla Cissé[45] are eliminated." Yet, Diallo has never expressed any claim for separatism or ethnic segregation. What he has done, though, is an appeal to more empathy and understanding with regards to how exactly Fula communities were becoming vulnerable to radical recruitment. He did say that had he been sixteen or seventeen, he would have rightfully taken up arms against the government,[46] as he could empathize with feelings of injustice of Fula herders from his background. This was deemed to be mild support and justification of jihadism, and not a call to understanding. Beyond Mali, Diallo has been touted as a Fula supremacist, feeding the overall narrative of dangerous Fula trying to dismantle modern states in order to rule over communities they deemed inferior, such as during the October 2016 Fula organizations conference in Ouagadougou. The conference aimed to discuss issues Fula communities were then confronted with throughout Africa. As we previously mentioned, Ali Nouhoum Diallo's positions were conflated with those of Cellou Dalein Diallo, he himself regularly depicted in racial terms as a dangerous supremacist, or as a "foreigner" as he was during his campaign for presidency in 2010. Leaders could hardly be allowed to express themselves fully in the name of their communities, for fear of being labeled as racists. Ethnicity is supposed to not be relevant, even as unrest is based on struggles that are specific to certain groups' very identity, history, and social memory. Thus, a political and community leader such as Ali Nouhoum Diallo may be silenced or despised based on the belief that his identity-based advocacy is a danger to national identity. This, in turn, creates the impression for Fula that their advocates are afraid or powerless. In the specific case of Ali Nouhoum Diallo, he did not relent, persisted.

The idea that Ali Nouhoum Diallo was in league with Fula extremist movements that sought to destabilize Mali only has partial roots in his advocacy for herders of Douentza. One other probable cause for this narrative may be Diallo's proposition of inclusive talks with Amadou Kouffa, the leader of the former Katiba Ansar Dine Macina (previously the front for the Liberation of Macina). Diallo had proposed talks with Kouffa with the aim of bringing Fula combatants allied to jihadists movements to put down their arms. This was met by no decisive support from the government. Kouffa communicated through official edicts in 2017 (some of them online) that Diallo was not an interlocutor for him, as he believed him to be a "slave of France and the West." Diallo further explained that his proposition was a sincere attempt at exploring peaceful means of bringing an end to violence. In a dangerously sensitive context of polarized stances on peacekeeping, attempts of discussions were met with suspicion, with ambivalent discourses from Malian political leaders. On the one hand, the national 2017 conference organized by the government of Mali to reach out to various components of Malian societies and most notably personalities involved in tensions in the north, prescribed that talks should be had with jihadists. The minister of national reconciliation, Mohamed El Moctar, himself supported that idea.[47] On the other hand, the president of Mali, Ibrahim Boubacar Keita, announced less than a year later, in February 2018, that talks with jihadists were out of the question.[48]

The greater narrative of the war on terrorism was never too far away from discussions, with continuous drive from international partners to make the Sahel a safe space in order to defuse jihadist recruitment and activities in other regions such as Europe or coastal West Africa. These narratives' social preeminence certainly contributed to a "rally around the flag" effect and polarization of public opinions around the question of terror and terrorism. These words come to mean very little more than slogans and brand vocabulary. No one knew exactly who is a terrorist, and how to define terrorists. Global understanding of terrorists conflates them with jihadists. Because of that, when President Keita mentioned negotiations with jihadists, it is still unclear who exactly is being considered. After the signature of the Algiers Agreements in June 2015, rebel groups joined the clout of Malian power and politics. There was at one point a proposal to erase crimes committed in the context of the crisis started in 2012.[49] For those groups or individuals that had taken up arms against the state, this would represent a tremendous opportunity for pardon. It would however deepen the feeling of injustice by victims. Regarding narratives about Fula victimhood, this would further the idea that no justice is obtainable and that the state was giving way for domination by armed groups that victimized in the past and that were then masters of the land and legitimate before the international community because of the Algiers Agreements and their proximity to the power in Bamako. For fighters in the bush, what to hope, then? Who was the true terrorist?

Though then-Malian prime minister Soumeylou Boubeye Maïga asserted during a speech in April 2018[50] that crimes against humanity, sexual crimes, and crimes that could not fall under statutes of limitation would not be included within those acts that would be pardoned, there was little reassurance that victims and their communities of attachment would be placated. The issue of justice for victims of the Malian army was still majorly missing. With recognized leaders like Ali Nouhoum Diallo silenced and intimidated, it seemed difficult to find hope in the civil society which still needed to be the principal partner of the government, unlike armed groups that were trying to broker collaboration on terms that would further deny justice.

With the idea that military collaboration could be a way into conflict resolution, a major figure such as General Ismaïla Cissé must be considered. It is notable that in 2016, Malian authorities had proposed to integrate some Fulani fighters into the DDR[51] process. On June 25, 2016, the leader of the Platform of Self-Defense Groups,[52] Harouna Toureh, announced that Fula fighters would be joining the ranks of the Platform, amid mass dissention among Fula communities. One Fula civil society leader warned us at the time that this was a pure political move by Fula elites in order to ingratiate political leaders of Bamako, since the Platform was backed by the Malian government. That person felt that the civil society had reached it limits. Other leaders among whom General Ismaïla Cissé—a founding member of Tabital Pulaaku International, and a highly admired figure within the Fula diaspora because of his Fula patronage and his illustrious and rare position as a Fula high-ranking soldier—explained that Fula fighters needed to be put into a legitimate fold. Integrating the Platform would be a gateway to DDR for Fula groups that were neither recognized by the Malian government nor the international community, and that did not sign the Algiers Agreements. Because of these factors, these armed groups would allegedly not be willing to put down their arms without guarantees. These fighters were from various backgrounds. It remains unclear to what extent they were "jihadists" and how many of them had connections with Kouffa's movement. The way the process of discussion with the Platform was presented, though, signaled that fighters needed some form of and shows of goodwill from the Malian government. This was about bringing back into the fold children of the nation who had been led astray but who were then willing to make amends. That idea had been the general stance pushed by Malian leaders since the time of the political transition in 2012 and 2013: children of Mali were to be considered for negotiations, but foreign fighters and jihadists who did not have a place in the narrative of a united Malian national family were to be met with harshness. With this approach, Malian citizens could be satiated in their desire for firmness with aggressors, all the while, Malian authorities were showing they could be flexible and they were not warmongers nor were they lusting for absolute vengeance.

In these times, Hamma Foune Diallo announced the creation of the MDP[53] on June 25, 2016.[54] An experienced fighter, Hamma Foune as he is simply known, fought in Mali against rebels in the early 1990s, during the great Tamasheq rebellion. He also fought in Sierra Leone during the country's civil war. Hamma Foune is said to have also fought alongside the MNLA in 2012, though that remains to be clearly proven. In 2016, when talks began about Fula fighters joining the Platform, he was hailed as a powerful holder of sway with rural fighters who were weary of facing the Malian government and wanted a way into reintegration. His men and himself numbered somewhere between 200 and 500 depending on reports. The narrative that circulated at the time was that these were youths who had been seduced by Kouffa and his allies from Al-Qaeda-affiliated movements, and who were now ready to serve their one country, Mali, in an efficient way. These fighters were depicted as humble youths who simply wanted to protect their people and their lands from aggressions by other communities, from cattle robbery, army oppression, and so on. Attempts to join the Platform would have to empower them and enable them to operationalize their desire to be helpful, in a lawful framework. Hamma Foune was never quite convincing. He came back into the fold of Bamako, but his sway proved to not have been as it was narrated. At the time, even within Tabital Pulaaku and other powerful civil society Fula organizations, the idea that Fula voices would melt into greater organizations was met with quite some wariness. No organization so far had been capable of vying successfully for Fula plights. The allure of recognition for the MDP and various smaller Fula bands did not seem to outweigh the dangers of recuperation of Fula voices by larger movements. Moreover, the GATIA,[55] a member of the Platform, had been tangled in violent conflicts with Fula both in Douentza Cercle in far-eastern Mali, along the border with Niger. Indeed, the prospect of Fula fighters having to serve under GATIA leadership was daunting. Ultimately, the integration project fell short with no further commitments by Malian political leaders, and after various mishaps between the GATIA and Fula civilians as well as armed groups of Fula persuasion. For instance, during the time of the talks presided by Harouna Toureh about integrating Fula fighters into the Platform, on June 11, 2016, rivalries between the GATIA and another component of the Platform, Ganda Izo, led to the GATIA attacking a Fula congregation in Douentza region with firearms.[56] Cattle and various goods were pilfered. Several Fula were killed and wounded. Ever since, no conclusive rapprochement endeavors to integrate Fula people into the DRR process have been materialized. It could be argued that some of the movements within the Platform are decidedly Fula movements. Ganda Koy and Ganda Izo, both part of the CMFPR[57] aisle of the Platform, are made up of Fula fighters in a very sizable portion. However, it must be considered that Fula communities in these groups, though proudly Fula, are little concerned with Fula identity-based politics at the national or the international level. Living in Fula enclaves surrounded by Songhay people, such as Gabero, near Gao, they have been historical allies of various communities of the area at some point or other in history.[58] However, past Tamasheq rebellions have resulted in traumatic reactions that led to violent uprisings in these Fula communities of the north of Mali. A local martial culture was born, with lasting antagonism toward Tamasheq, and natural lasting alliances with Songhay fighters. Fighters of Ganda Koy,[59] a member of CMFPR, were among those militias accused of mass killings of Arab and Tamasheq civilians during the rebellions of the early 1990s. Ganda Izo,[60] a latter offshoot of Gandz Koy, is also a member of the CMFPR. Given past contexts of their call to arms, Fula in these movements did not have distinctly Fula voices in their actions.

General Ismaila Cissé, for all his fame and purported sway, was not able to mobilize Fula leaders to serve his idea of integrating Fula into the national army in order to have them defend their own heartlands with legitimacy and power. Though General Cissé was associated with several attempts of negotiation with armed groups, liberations of hostages, defusing dangerous situations in the center of Mali, his lack of political power and his chilly relations with then-rulers of Mali ultimately disabled his efforts. A native of Konza, in historical Macina, General Ismaïla Cissé was trained in Mali and Germany. He served as governor of the district of Bamako and gained renown throughout the Fula diaspora. His physical appearance, redolent of classical Fula archetypes, is often cited as a token of his "Fulaness." During the conference, we attended in 2013 in Ouagadougou, praise-singers were insistent on his properness to lead Fula.

Similarly, to Ali Nouhoum Diallo, General Cissé is also often threatened. There have been media articles calling him a racist and a supremacist as well, in attempts to silence him. This constitutes grounds for reflection on the possibility of pacifying social tensions in Mali so as to be able to benefit from local actors and leaders' abilities to solve problems and enable them to positively connect their communities with state initiatives. General Cissé was not able to change politics in Mali in a visible and lasting fashion. This is quite certainly evident that the country, at a systemic level, has been struggling to include community voices in the building of its resilience to terror and violent conflict.

Individuals could not rise to enact hope. And so, in-group expectations of individuals decreased, giving space to extremist rationales about Fula needing to quit victimhood for good and violently fight. This, in turn, contributed to dividing Fula individuals and groups, realizing a self-fulfilling idea that Fula were cursed with perpetual division and infighting. Numbers or successful individuals were not benefiting them. What then, to expect at a broad community-level? Who would save all? Who could, in such diversity of locations, contexts, situations? In the race for recruitment of sympathizers, it seems actors from the field have been put in the delicate position of facing a seemingly unsurmountable system of politics or compromising their ethics. It seems as if there truly were no more heroes.

Identity narratives, more often than not, trample other communities' assertion of their rights to exist and occupy lands and political scenes, as the narrative about the project of a powerful Dogon Country antagonizing other communities makes apparent. Proponents of the creation of an Islamic golden age as befits Quranic narratives alienate communities' ways of life and their pragmatic day-to-day means of handling production and alleviating their harsh conditions of life, as is the case when coalitions of jihadists appear and restrict movements for women and try to dictate immutable and rigorist behaviors to people unaccustomed to their alien ways. State-led nationalistic narratives have a coarse tendency to devalue legitimate claims based on suffering and victimhood, always pushing forward discourses on sacrifice for the greater good.

Leaders vie for political initiatives in the name of people whose true aggregated opinions remain largely unknown and unfathomable. Researchers, such as ourselves—a marginal actor—too, can only rely on observable trends and public relations operations in order to ascertain what exactly it is that the majority of people wish. Victimhood and suffering have become commodities that are summoned to strengthen narratives and justify war, search for support and resources, legitimacy. With broken hero narratives in the midst of broader ever-evolving violent contexts, there exists even lesser spaces for community initiatives for peace.

NOTES

1. Dupire, 1970.
2. Fula in Mali and Guinea's transborder Wasulu region are wont to be heard boasting, "we are the noble Fula folk who do not speak Fula." Our own paternal grandmother, a noble Fula from Xaaso, used to say, "Us, we are not *mbiimi* Fula." *Mbiimi* means "I say" in Fula. It is a phrase often used by Fula speakers at the onset of declarations. In our grandmother's mind, this related to a certain type of Fula very close to stereotypically ancient Fula traditions like cattle herding, close-knit endogamy, and monolingualism in a Fula tongue.
3. Angola, Belgium, France, Japan, United States, and so on.
4. Pulaaku also refers to all Fula people, the assembly of peoples of Fula origin. It is to be understood as a unifying term that trumps even castes.
5. This idea is based on the narrative that Fula are physically different from all their neighbors (Dogon, Tamasheq, Bamanan, Wolof, Yoruba, etc.) because of a specific ancestral genesis.
6. Konaré, 2011.
7. Popular stories would have Fula people come from as far away as India, millennia ago, because of their physical appearance and their ways of favoring cows, as Hindus do.
8. There are attempts to standardize Fula languages into a modern standard Fula language, notwithstanding the richness and diversity that Fula people enjoy in practicing their native tongues, which are all usually inter-intelligible.
9. In Fula language, this means "One people, one language."
10. For instance, during an external meeting we organized in Dakar, on November 12, 2017, at the onset of the Dakar Forum for Peace and Security in Africa, debates became heated. Mali's PARENA (a political party) leader Tiébilé Dramé pondered whether the birth of ethnicity-centered organizations such as Tabital Pulaaku was not one of the causes of tensions between communities. He wondered whether presenting problems of insecurity as problems between communities was not charging situations with community elements which they did not initially possess, and thus advertising narratives of essential differences between peoples.
11. In March 2017, a state officer from a neighboring country told us: Organizations like Tabital Pulaaku that say they are global, they are spreading their tentacles

all over our countries, trying to sow division among us. They say that they defend Fula, but they are only instilling paranoia and defiance in our fellow countrymen's minds.

12. Douentza is a cercle in the center of the country. Its namesake, the city of Douentza, is a major pole of activity in the vicinity. Fula are the majority in the area, though Songhay, Dogon, Bozos, Bamanan, and Tamasheq also live there. Douentza hosts a military camp, schools, and clinics. The city was notably abandoned by the Malian army in March 2012 before invaders even attacked. When invaders did come, they were in the form of the MNLA, not the jihadists of Al-Qaeda-affiliated Ansar Dine. Douentza was greatly looted, and its local elites were forced to flee. Pillaging, rapes, and everyday acts of injustice by the rebels were universally reported, though the MNLA always failed to take responsibility. That attitude of the occupying forces led to important unpopularity, such that when the MUJWA appeared during the summer of 2012, it was able to enlist the help of numerous youths who ultimately contributed to ousting the rebels. After the MUJWA took over, traditional elites became even more threatened, as the movement was jihadist and socially revolutionary. The MUJWA and its proponents accused local elites of fostering corruption and appropriating power and resources from more vulnerable fringes of the population such as herders. Though both herders and elites are of Fula extraction, rivalries between them were rife with discourses about injustice and no redistribution of wealth. With elites collaborating with the ailing state of Mali, they were considered to be causes of the downfall of the area. Past frustrations over land ownership and access to development also resurfaced. Moreover, Douentza being formally part of the "south," and with road networks leaving it out of the main humanitarian axis linking urban areas of the north, denizens of the area were never able to benefit from sizable relief sent from the narrated "south" to the narrated "north." The overall ecological dryness and lack of strategic value (then) of Douentza ensured that it was one of the areas geographically closest to the start of the liberation to be reached by the coalition led by Malian soldiers. Thus, the MUJWA's discourse about the people of Douentza being abandoned victims became stronger as the movement was fleeing the city.

13. For instance, the upheaval caused by hunters in the center of Mali certainly had roots in neighboring countries where hunter militias have been gaining fighting experience for years. Moreover, as we have tried to explain previously in this work, global trends and global phenomena have clear impacts on very local contexts (the war in Libya, among others).

14. Konaré, 2011.
15. Diallo, 2014.
16. Lam, 1993.
17. Singular: Baleejo. This means "a black person." It refers to dark-skinned non-Fula. It is not to be taken to mean that a Fula cannot be dark-hued, though it used to imply that Fula are not part of the greater family of Blacks. However, with global narratives on blackness and awareness of blackness, Fula we interviewed during prior studies were insistent that Baleejo does not exclusively refer to the color of skin, though it is used as a describer related to this. One interviewee notably told us, "we use this term to differentiate between ourselves and foreigners because as Fula we

are pure of race, and like milk." In that sense, Baleeɓe is close to Haaɓe, as a way of referring to non-Fula.

18. Our mother is the "founding and lifetime patron" of Tabital Pulaaku, and we had formally represented her publicly four months prior at an international Tabital Pulaaku event in August 2013, in Burkina Faso.

19. Alerte sur la préparation du génocide contre les Peuls et le projet de guerre civile en Moyenne Guinée lancé par le président Alpha Condé. (September 22, 2013). Retrieved from https://actuguinee.org/index.php/2013/09/22/alerte-sur-la-prepara tion-du-genocide-contre-les-peuls-et-le-projet-de-guerre-civile-en-moyenne-guinee -lance-par-le-president-alpha-conde/.

20. There is evidence that Fula were targeted because of their ethnicity during a crackdown in a stadium in Conakry where opposition leaders were denouncing the junta in charge, on September 28, 2009. Guinea: Stadium Massacre, Rape Likely Crimes Against Humanity (December 17, 2009). Retrieved from https://www.hrw.org/news/2009/12/17/guinea-stadium-massacre-rape-likely-crimes-against-hum anity.

21. Alhassane Condé (he went on to become President Alpha Condé's minister of territory administration and decentralization), in charge of public relations for then presidential candidate Alpha Condé said, speaking of Fula candidate Cellou Dalein Diallo: "Cellou and his militants can go to Somalia." That is if he was discontent. Somalia, like Ethiopia, are countries imagined to be the "real" homeland of Fula. For outside observers, such words may seem innocuous, but they deeply echo intercommunity insecurity and trigger anxiety in social memory given the alienation of Fula as being foreigners in various parts of Africa, due to their expansion and history of migrations.

22. Lam, 1993.

23. For instance, many discussions took place about the origins of Fula, differences in dialects, or the polysemy of some Fula words. Contributors range from laypersons to famed academics.

24. As opposed to people who were known, and who could be identified.

25. A person trying to provoke reactions, on the Internet.

26. Former president of the national assembly in Mali.

27. Opposition leader in Guinea.

28. Such was the case in July 2018, in Washington, DC, when Malian authorities downplayed the importance of a march by Fula diaspora members to protest against the victimization of Fula in Mali as an action by foreigners who did not understand the Malian context.

29. These figures went on to be highly disseminated. Troup Buchanan, R. (November 18, 2015). The fourth most deadly terror group that you've never heard of. Retrieved from https://www.independent.co.uk/news/world/africa/global-terro rism-index-nigerian-fulani-militants-named-as-fourth-deadliest-terror-group-in-w orld-a6739851.html.

30. Internationally celebrated intellectuals such as Wole Soyinka have participated in this. Herdsmen killings: Buhari dey sleep on top bicycle. Wole Soyinka (February 13, 2018). Retrieved July 05, 2020, from https://www.bbc.com/pidgin/tori-43041267.

31. Koné, 2018.
32. Ibid.
33. Koné, 2016.
34. Pluralism is the expression of multiple possibilities stemming from a situation of diversity.
35. August-September 2015.
36. United Nations definition of "Indigenous Peoples": "Considering the diversity of indigenous peoples, an official definition of 'indigenous' has not been adopted by any UN-system body. Instead the system has developed a modern understanding of this term based on the following: • Self-identification as indigenous peoples at the individual level and accepted by the community as their member. • Historical continuity with pre-colonial and/or pre-settler societies • Strong link to territories and surrounding natural resources • Distinct social, economic or political systems • Distinct language, culture and beliefs • Form non-dominant groups of societies • Resolve to maintain and reproduce their ancestral environments and systems as distinctive peoples and communities."

This indicates how diversity and access to power signify indigenous status. It should not be understood as meaning that one group arrived in an area first, and is thus "more indigenous" than another. Hence, Fula can be a numerous community long settled somewhere and yet still retain indigenous status. This also depends on which specific subgroup of Fula is considered. In on our current mention of the term, we aim to convey the thought that plurality of minority experiences did not appear to be of major import in our experience.

Indigenous Peoples, Indigenous Peoples: Factsheet. (n.d.). Retrieved July 12, 2020, from https://www.un.org/esa/socdev/unpfii/documents/5session_factsheet1.pdf.

37. Her five-year term lasted for six years: from 2007 to 2013, since 2012 to 2013 was an extra-term year due to the coup d'état in Bamako and the political transition.
38. FAMA refers to the Malian army, from French "Forces Armées du Mali" (Armed Forces of Mali). It also means "power holder, wealthy" in Bamanan and Maninka, Mande languages.
39. A former minister, governor general of the capital city, and a key member of ADEMA-PASJ (Alliance pour la Démocratie au Mali-Parti Africain pour la Solidarité et la Justice, one of Mali's top political parties in terms of parliament seats and arguably the most reliable political machine given its track record of victory over the years). In the years leading to the Malian presidential elections of 2018, she was most notably a leader of a multiparty movement against an unpopular change of the Malian constitution in 2017. The movement was a success and repealed the government project of a new decried constitution.
40. The Economic Community of West African States.
41. Noble folks, yet with no ruling power, in the first tier of castes.
42. Initially, Ali Nouhoum Diallo was depicted as a wise old man who wished to negotiate with Jihadists. Abba, S. (August 30, 2017). Alioune Nouhoum Diallo, le patriarche malien qui veut raisonner le djihadiste Amadou Koufa. Retrieved from

https://www.lemonde.fr/afrique/article/2017/08/30/alioune-nouhoum-diallo-le-patriarche-malien-qui-veut-raisonner-le-djihadiste-amadou-koufa_5178636_3212.html.

43. Tounkara, 2017.

44. Sangaré, 2016.

45. A high-ranking officer, and former ambassador of Mali Equatorial Guinea.

46. Ali Nouhoum Diallo's interview, in saying that he would have taken up arms if he had been 16 or 17, was met with controversy. https://niarela.net/interviews/pr-ali-nouhoum-diallo-si-javais-16-ou-17-ans-aujourdhui-je-prendrai-les-armes.

47. The national conference publicly raised the question of whether or not negotiating with jihadists was a necessity. http://www.rfi.fr/afrique/20170403-mali-conference-entente-nationale-dialoguer-Jihadistes.

48. The president did not initially wish to negotiate with jihadists. Ayad, C., Tilouine, J., & Kpatindé, F. (February 22, 2018). Ibrahim Boubacar Keïta: "Pas question de négocier avec les djihadistes." Retrieved from https://www.lemonde.fr/afrique/article/2018/02/22/ibrahim-boubacar-keita-pas-question-de-negocier-avec-les-djihadistes_5260800_3212.html.

49. The controversy surrounding government attempts at new legislation highlighted difficulties of the government to manage religious leaders of the country. Le Cam, M. (June 8, 2018). Au Mali, un projet de loi d'entente nationale qui suscite la controverse. Retrieved from https://www.lemonde.fr/afrique/article/2018/06/08/au-mali-un-projet-de-loi-d-entente-nationale-qui-suscite-la-controverse_5311887_3212.html.

50. The Malian prime minister declared that the government did not consider the integration of ex-rebels to still be a matter to manage. Ahmed, B. (April 23, 2018). Mali: L'intégration des ex-rebelles est une question " résolue," affirme le Premier ministre—Jeune Afrique. Retrieved from http://www.jeuneafrique.com/553498/politique/mali-lintegration-des-ex-rebelles-est-une-question-resolue-affirme-le-premier-ministre/.

51. Disarmament, Demobilization and Reintegration (DDR). (February 15, 2015). Retrieved from https://minusma.unmissions.org/en/disarmament-demobilization-and-reintegration-ddr.

52. This group was formally created at the onset of the formal application of the Algiers Agreements, in June 2015, in order to promote the common goals of those armed groups that signed the Algiers Agreements viewing themselves as being "pro-government" and committing to that idea. They are generally opposed, in discourses, to the CMA—the Coordination of the Movements of Azawad. While the "Platform" is quite heterogeneous in terms of communities represented within (Songhay, Tamasheq, Fula in Songhay areas, Arabs), the CMA is entirely made up of Arab and Tamasheq groups. Daou, B. (June 27, 2016). Processus de paix au Mali: Le MDP adhère à la Plateforme et invite l'Etat à sécuriser les personnes et leurs biens Processus de paix au Mali: Le MDP adhère à la Plateforme et invite l'Etat à sécuriser les personnes et leurs biens. Retrieved from http://malijet.com/a_la_une_du_mali/159219-processus_paix_mdp_adhere_plateforme.html.

53. Mouvement pour la Défense de la Patrie—Movement for the Defense of the Fatherland.

54. Hama Foune Diallo proved difficult to depict, as he had quite the eclectic background. Carayol, R. (July 18, 2016). Mali: Hama Foune Diallo, mercenaire du delta—Jeune Afrique. Retrieved from http://www.jeuneafrique.com/mag/340339/politique/mali-hama-foune-diallo-mercenaire-delta/.

55. The GATIA had been one of the single most powerful armed groups in Mali, owing in large part to General Alhadji Ag Gamou, a high-ranking officer of the Mali army originating from the Imghad community of Tamasheq, spreading out from Motpi region in Mali all the way to Niger. General Alhadji Ag Gamou is famed as one of the liberators of the north of Mali after rebel attacks and jihadist domination. His unit which was comprised of Tamasheq fighters retreated to Niger through then-Gao region and held their ground during several skirmishes with rebel groups and jihadists movements for months. At the time of the liberation of the north of Mali, he went back to Mali with his fighters and was welcomed as a war hero, although he had been a subject of racist smear campaigns in early 2012, when many in the public opinion assumed that he had ran away to Niger and was defecting to join fellow Tamasheq and aid rebels. These analyzes failed to take into account the fact that Alhadji Ag Gamou had his own agendas, and that what is viewed as a monolithic Tamasheq people is really an amazing ensemble of tribes, lineages, and castes with complex dynamics. Alhadji Ag Gamou's Imghad community are a people who are not traditionally considered to be bonded, and who may possess land and cattle, but who were not considered to be a prestigious people by some other Tamasheq. The fight of Alhadji Ag Gamou has been in many ways a fight for Imghad rise. This narrative is quite popular with hawkish Tamasheq aristocrats who contend that the Imghad lack nobility and that they have hidden agendas of asserting their power in defiant and vengeful manners over other Tamasheq. GATIA went on to become a usual suspect in violence against civilians in central and northern Mali, as well as in western Niger.

56. Attempts at mediation were publicized, although they ultimately failed. Rfi. (June 13, 2016). Mali: Tentative de conciliation après les affrontements de Douentza. Retrieved from http://www.rfi.fr/afrique/20160613-mali-tentative-conciliation-apres-affrontements-douentza.

57. Coordination des Mouvements et Front Patriotique de Résistance (Coordination of Movements and Patriotic Resistance Front).

58. Grémont, 2005.

59. Master of the Land, in Songhay language.

60. Children of the Land, in Songhay language.

Conclusion

In this brief work, we have tried to demonstrate the many ways through which identity is utilized to fuel political strategies at a community level. We have intended to describe narrative factors at play in conflict engagement. We have purposefully made the choice to not bring forth quantitative data that may account for narrative-based conflict resolution. The lack of chronological distance at the time of writing made it difficult to assess the efficiency of narrative-based political strategies in war in our region of interest. Paradigms were changing, and there was massive social exhaustion due to an exceeding use of symbolism to fabricate peace.

In contemporary Malian contexts, trust in narratives has been tenuous and it does not seem as if the age of the Internet and mass dissemination of information, narratives, and shock content, is contributing to peacebuilding in meaningful ways. Most contemporary narratives revolve around the appraisal of suffering and its evaluation for each community when confronted with others communities' very own struggles. Community-level resilience is put to the test, and divided communities fail to create endogenous solutions, contributing to polarization. With no support from internal figures and narratives that they may lean on and no comforting wider national narratives, communities are threatened by the appeal of extremisms. Activists on the Internet, public figures, community organizations, in advocating for their own groups, push forward experimental strategies of rebirth. Thus, in the midst of internal narratives breaning up, they would rather rely on remnants of inner self, rather than subscribing to wider narratives, in search for inner revival. Those wider narratives come with insecurity and mistrust based on failures of government narratives. This conundrum makes one ponder how to find a balance between identifying with downtrodden marginal people's plights and working with governments and other groups in a way that creates lasting counterproductive tension?

This work has been but a brief cut into Fula stakes and group perceptions of violent conflict in a specific Malian context. It is our belief that nation-building and group identity-building are factors that play into the kindling of group-wide defiance and contestation.

In Mali, ancient state narratives are employed to foster a sense of unity that is put to the test every day, as violence keeps erupting and rising. As grand and beautiful as the idea of Mali as a nation-state has been that narrative leaves victims of atrocities and injustice very jaded. Narratives that purport to be positive and unite the people sometimes contribute to mistrust and division. State narratives have ended up appearing not only as public relations stories to artificially conjure calm and unity, but more and more as sophisticated ploys to placate the people and to outsmart them into preserving power for a small political elite.

Just as narratives of domination have allowed royal lines throughout Mali to perpetuate their legitimacy over the people of the areas their ancestors ruled over, narratives of national integration are now plotting Malian history with multiple instances of forceful exercise of power. That past is nowadays romanticized with chronological distance. With discourses that posit that leaders are making sacrifices, chasing terrorists, unifying the land under a righteous unitary rule, what is unfolding, really, is the subjugation of communities and the erasure of their voices as communities.

Currently, in a time of quick communication of information, the longer erasure of community voices goes on, the more communities harshly reject state interference as they become knowledgeable about. Just as MNLA supporters mocked Mali and its narratives as "fairy tales," some Fula came to view political endeavors of Mali as sham or utter failure, with every shocking news coming from their brethren in distant areas. There is little room for nuance after polarization and extreme defeat. With no hopes of justice and security, narratives of victimhood, though depressing, are embraced, in a search for cataclysmic change. These changes that are wished for seem almost as legendary as tales of the Pax Mali and Grand Imperial Mali. Fantasied countries ruled only by Fula are brought up in discussions, as well as safe heavens with pastures aplenty, the use of Pulaaku values to uphold social values and peace, and so on. Considering the process of imagining a materialized Fula nation, idealization of the in-group serves a function of psychological soothing. This process of co-creation acts as sublimation, conversion of negative thoughts, like art unfolding, to bring succor in times of despair. Narratives are held on to create hope and journeys that give meaning to life. Why live with no endgame, in a failing country? This is true for all peoples of Mali. Despair is a constant. Faced with great despondency, the alleviation of sorrow takes the form of groupthink and group creation. Groups are not a congregation of beings, nor are they specifically an addition of ideals shared. Groups share, in the words of Kaes (2015), a group psychic device. This great emotional tool is made up of feelings of belonging together and being owned by each other. How a group may be precisely defined means little. As in the case of Fula, delineations are blurry. It remains impossible to reach a consensus on who exactly is a Fula, depending on the context in which that question is being posed. What is more tangible is self-affirmation and assertive behaviors of identity.

Fula people, or Malians general, or descendants of ancient Mande, all may benefit from emotional devices that they co-construct through daily nourishment of their ideas of belonging together. In this day and age, writing online, subscribing to a social media group, buying merchandise from members of the community, all become assertions of identity and help in sustaining the psychic existence of identity. The Fula psychic device that we have encountered during years of observation is made up of ancient narratives about "Fulaness," use of stereotypes in order to allow for everyone to know how to perform group identity. By asserting claim to Fula identity, by performing in ways that are deemed legitimate for a Fula, and by repeating narratives heard, group identity is practiced and nourished every day, in various locales. Geographical and genetic distance matter little. Then, as a group, Fula people express themselves from a common pool of ideas and feelings, however different and disconnected. They empathize with violent revolt, pacific advocacy, cultural entrepreneurship, arts, and so on. The same fundamental slogans of unity are conveyed, and there is never any doubt about narratives summoned. In this, the idea that Fula people are united is quite evident. And yet, struggles are different, personal experiences, though quickly amalgamated into one another ultimately make it impossible for strategic narratives to create utopias. General Cissé wished for integration of Fula fighters into the platform. This was rejected by individual wills that, while supporting the same narratives of the "Tragic Fula Isolation" or "Fula Extermination," did not believe in what they viewed as submitting to union without agency or justice. Nuance is ever needed. Those Fula people who joined jihadists remain related to Fula civilians of their regions. Individual circumstances have canceled attempts of recruitment by jihadists in Fula communities partly because of difficult articulation between jihadist narratives and dogmas, and *Fula Freedom in Social Life*.[1] Unity is wished for, freedom is essential. The lack of union between Fula people is often lamented and told of in a narrative of tragedy, as one other identity marker of Fula folks: forever condemned to be divided while being so many and displaying so much talent and beauty and overall blessing. Group narratives create ambivalent attachment. Fears of Fula nationalism need to be unpacked with nuance, too. As we have often noted in this work, Fula people come with diverse agendas, sociologies, and positions. Truly, Fula people are diverse in their homogeneity. Attempts to belong together are indeed contributing to trends of transnational collaboration that rely on emotions as a vital driver. Yet, the violence of bad governance, alienating narratives, daily economic and physical vulnerability, is causing more traction in mobilizing Fula people into violent conflicts than narratives have. When they join fights, they join not because of narratives that have fed and inhabited them for decades. They do so for a much more fundamental and urgent reason: to survive.

In constructing strategic narratives to bring peace, it is of capital import that new models be considered. If the very idea of narratives could be considered as a tool for peacebuilding, as opposed to convenient ex-nihilo stories to be summoned for ad hoc instances, then, surely, it should be allowed that we think more concertation and co-construction would be beneficial to all. If we agree that narratives aren't just made-up stories we utilize, then we should give them more consideration. Fula communities in Mali have developed in-group narratives. Actors external to Fula communities have developed narratives about Fula people. The intersection of narratives that positively resonate with Fula communities and narratives that serve great security strategies can be supported with good concertation. Through our interviews, studies, and experiences, we have witnessed firsthand the eagerness of Malians of all communities and social backgrounds in wanting to belong to a narrative of power and lasting protection. When interests are transparently laid out and promises are kept, hope is possible. As flawed as cooperation between Mali and Algiers Agreement signatory groups was, their shared narrative of the necessary union for peace and against terrorism brought a boost in international tactical support and financial gains by signatory armed groups. From governments of Mali's perspective, they could show their alliances with these groups as a token of goodwill. Surely, invitations to participate in discussions that can materialize progressively built narratives may be extended to others. There needs to be honest and rigorous endeavors in hearing all voices and taking vows of co-constructing narratives. However well designed any partnership and its storytelling are, deception and injustice never seem to pay off in the long run.

If any lesson should be learned from this work, we insist that it be about how the responsibility to listen to narratives and to aid and protect victims is much more liberating and pragmatically useful than perpetual remembrance of dated narratives, and participation in processes of othering victims by excluding them from rigid narratives. There is power in being a group, even in diversity and with the power of diversity. Narratives are ever-evolving. It will always be possible to perfect them.

NOTE

1. Here, we are citing Paul Riesman's book title (1998). In his engrossing scientific narrative, Paul Riesman cleverly describes how Fula societies mold individuals into hardened and stoic adults, in order to better achieve independence and safety in freedom as they enjoy the benefits and the paradoxical hardships of life in the bush. Life in the bush is a life of freedom for herders.

References

Abba, Seidik. "Alioune Nouhoum Diallo, Le Patriarche Malien Qui Veut Raisonner Le DJihadiste Amadou Koufa." Le Monde.fr. Le Monde, August 30, 2017. https://www.lemonde.fr/afrique/article/2017/08/30/alioune-nouhoum-diallo-le-patriarche-malien-qui-veut-raisonner-le-dJihadiste-amadou-koufa_5178636_3212.html.
"Accord D'Alger Pour La Restauration De La Paix, De La Sécurité Et Du Développement Dans La Région De Kidal | UN Peacemaker." United Nations. United Nations, July 4, 2006. https://peacemaker.un.org/mali-accordalger2006.
AFP. "Au Sénégal, Le Président Macky Sall Accusé D'avoir 'Insulté La Mémoire Des Tirailleurs'." Le Monde, May 28, 2018. https://www.lemonde.fr/afrique/article/2018/05/28/au-senegal-le-president-macky-sall-accuse-d-avoir-insulte-la-memoire-des-tirailleurs_5305963_3212.html.
Ahmed, Baba. "Mali: L'intégration Des Ex-Rebelles Est Une Question 'Résolue', Affirme Le Premier Ministre – Jeune Afrique." JeuneAfrique.com. Jeune Afrique, April 23, 2018. http://www.jeuneafrique.com/553498/politique/mali-lintegration-des-ex-rebelles-est-une-question-resolue-affirme-le-premier-ministre/.
"Alerte Sur La Préparation Du Génocide Contre Les Peuls Et Le Projet De Guerre Civile En Moyenne Guinée Lancé Par Le Président Alpha Condé." Actuguinee.org, September 22, 2013. https://actuguinee.org/index.php/2013/09/22/alerte-sur-la-preparation-du-genocide-contre-les-peuls-et-le-projet-de-guerre-civile-en-moyenne-guinee-lance-par-le-president-alpha-conde/.
Amselle, Jean-Loup, and Elikia M'Bokolo. *Au Coeur De L'ethnie: Ethnies, Tribalisme Et État En Afrique*. Paris: La Découverte, 2009.
Ayad, Christophe, Joan Tilouine, and Francis Kpatindé. "Ibrahim Boubacar Keïta: 'Pas Question De Négocier Avec Les DJihadistes'." Le Monde.fr. Le Monde, February 22, 2018. https://www.lemonde.fr/afrique/article/2018/02/22/ibrahim-boubacar-keita-pas-question-de-negocier-avec-les-dJihadistes_5260800_3212.html.
Ba Konaré, Adame. *Dictionnaire Des Femmes célèbres Du Mali: (Des Temps Mythico-légendaires Au 26 Mars 1991); précédé D'une Analyse Sur Le rôle Et

L'image De La Femme Dans L'Histoire Du Mali. Bamako (Mali): Ed. Jamana, 1993.

Ba Konaré, Adam. *Sonni Ali Ber*. Niamey: Institut de recherches en sciences humaines, 1977.

Ba Konare, Dougoukolo Alpha Oumar. "En Afrique, Le Fantasme D'une 'Communauté Peule' Radicalisée." The Conversation, September 4, 2018. https://theconversation.com/en-afrique-le-fantasme-dune-communaute-peule-radicalisee-102276.

Ba Konare, Dougoukolo Alpha Oumar. "'Au Mali, Le Monstre Du Terrorisme Ethnique a Ôté plus De Vies Que Le Djihadisme'." Le Monde.fr. Le Monde, April 14, 2019. https://www.lemonde.fr/afrique/article/2019/04/14/au-mali-le-monstre-du-terrorisme-ethnique-a-ote-plus-de-vies-que-le-djihadisme_5450086_3212.html.

Ba Konaré, Dougoukolo Alpha Oumar. "Peuls Et Dogons Dans La Tourmente Au Mali: Histoire D'une Longue Relation Ambivalente." The Conversation, March 29, 2019. https://theconversation.com/peuls-et-dogons-dans-la-tourmente-au-mali-histoire-dune-longue-relation-ambivalente-114396.

Ba Konaré, Dougoukolo Alpha Oumar. "Entre Faux DJihadistes Et Faux Chasseurs Traditionnels, Les Civils Piégés Dans Le Centre Du Mali." The Conversation, October 22, 2018. https://theconversation.com/entre-faux-dJihadistes-et-faux-chasseurs-traditionnels-les-civils-pieges-dans-le-centre-du-mali-105181.

Ba Konaré, Dougoukolo Alpha Oumar. "Transmission Transgénérationnelle Et Identité Ethnique: Clinique Des Peuls d'Afrique Occidentale," 2013.

Baby, Mahamane. "13 Raisons Pour Élire IBK En 2013." Malijet Mahamane Baby: 13 raisons pour élire IBK en 2013 Bamako Mali, July 17, 2013. http://malijet.com/actualite-politique-au-mali/76971-mahamane-baby-13-raisons-pour-elire-ibk-en-2013.html.

Barry, Alpha Ousmane. *L'Épopée Peule Du Fuuta Jaloo*. Paris: Karthala, 2011.

Bâ Amadou-Hampâté. *L'empire Peul Du Macina*. Paris: Mouton, 1962.

Benjaminsen, Tor A., and Boubacar Ba. "Why Do Pastoralists in Mali Join Jihadist Groups? A Political Ecological Explanation." *The Journal of Peasant Studies* 46, no. 1 (2018): 1–20. https://doi.org/10.1080/03066150.2018.1474457.

Bennett-Smith, Meredith. "Meet The World's Richest Man." HuffPost. HuffPost, October 21, 2014. https://www.huffpost.com/entry/mansa-musa-worlds-richest-man-all-time_n_1973840.

Bolougbeu, Elisée. "'Nous N'accepterons plus D'être Massacrés Et Spoliés Dans Le Silence.'" Guineelibre. Guineelibre, August 1, 2011. http://guineelibre.over-blog.com/article-nous-n-accepterons-plus-d-etre-massacres-et-spolies-dans-le-silence-80649586.html.

Bourgeot, André. "Démocratie, Pouvoirs Et Chefferies." Bamadanet, February 19, 2014. http://bamada.net/democratie-pouvoirs-et-chefferies.

Bruijn, Mirjam De, Adamou Amadou, Elie Lewa Doksala, and Boucary Sangaré. "Mobile Pastoralists in Central and West Africa: between Conflict, Mobile Telephony and (Im)Mobility." *Revue Scientifique et Technique de l'OIE* 35, no. 2 (2016): 649–57. https://doi.org/10.20506/rst.35.2.2546.

Carayol, Rémi. "A La Frontière Entre Le Niger Et Le Mali, L'alliance Coupable De L'armée Française." Mediapart, November 29, 2018. https://www.mediapar

t.fr/journal/international/291118/la-frontiere-entre-le-niger-et-le-mali-l-alliance-c oupable-de-l-armee-francaise.

Carayol, Rémi. "Mali: Hama Foune Diallo, Mercenaire Du Delta – Jeune Afrique." JeuneAfrique.com. Jeune Afrique, July 18, 2016. http://www.jeuneafrique.com/ma g/340339/politique/mali-hama-foune-diallo-mercenaire-delta/.

Chronique satirique: l'amiral Ladji Bourama au sommet sur la sécurité maritime, October 18, 2016. https://bamada.net/chronique-satirique-lamiral-ladji-bourama-au-sommet-sur-la-securite-maritime.

Cisse, Modibo Galy. "Hamadoun Koufa, Fer De Lance Du Radicalisme Dans Le Mali Central." *Biographies de la Radicalisation*, 2018, 181–202. https://doi.org/10.2307/j.ctvh9vtbr.14.

Cissoko Sékéné Mody. *Contribution à L'histoire Politique Du Khasso Dans Le Haut-Sénégal: Des Origines à 1854*. Paris: L'Harmattan, 1986.

"Commission, Vérité, Justice Et Réconciliation." n.d. http://cvjrmali.com/.

"The Concept of Pluralism: Media Diversity." Mediamonitor.nl, September 30, 2013. https://www.mediamonitor.nl/english/the-concept-of-pluralism-media-diversity/.

"Conférence D'entente Nationale Au Mali: Dialoguer Avec Les Jihadistes." RFI. RFI, April 3, 2017. http://www.rfi.fr/afrique/20170403-mali-conference-entente-nationale-dialoguer-Jihadistes.

Daou, Boukary. "Processus De Paix Au Mali: Le MDP Adhère à La Plateforme Et Invite l'Etat à Sécuriser Les Personnes Et Leurs Biens Processus De Paix Au Mali: Le MDP Adhère à La Plateforme Et Invite l'Etat à Sécuriser Les Personnes Et Leurs Biens." Le Républicain Mali. Malijet, June 27, 2016. http://malijet.com/a_la_une_du_mali/159219-processus_paix_mdp_adhere_plateforme.html.

Delafosse, Maurice. *Haut – Sénégal – Niger: (Soudan Français): 1. Série: Le Pays, Les Peuples, Les Langues, L'Histoire, Les Civilisations*. 1. Vol. 1. Paris: Hachette Livre, 1912.

Diallo, Bilguissa. *Guinée, 22 Novembre 1970*. Paris: Editions l'Harmattan, 2014.

Diallo, Ousmane Aly. "Ethnic Clashes, Jihad, and Insecurity in Central Mali." *Peace Review* 29, no. 3 (2017): 299–306. https://doi.org/10.1080/10402659.2017.1344529.

Dupire, Marguerite. *Organisation Sociale Des Peul: étude D'ethnographie comparée*. Paris: Librairie Plon, 1970.

Eliade, Mircea. *Mythes, Rêves Et Mystères*. Paris: Gallimard, 2016.

Gordon, Andrew J. "Cultural Identity and Illness: Fulani Views." *Cultural, Medicine, and Psychiatry* 24 (August 2000): 297–330.

Grémont, Charles. "Comment Les Touaregs Ont Perdu Le Fleuve." *Patrimoines naturels au Sud*, January 2005, 237–90. https://doi.org/10.4000/books.irdeditions.4066.

"Guerre Au Mali: Retour Sur Le Drame D'Aguelhok – Jeune Afrique." JeuneAfrique.com. Jeune Afrique, October 21, 2013. https://www.jeuneafrique.com/167687/politique/guerre-au-mali-retour-sur-le-drame-d-aguelhok/.

Guichaoua, Yvan, and Dougoukolo Alpha Oumar Ba Konaré. "Central Mali Gripped by a Dangerous Brew of Jihad, Revolt and Self-Defence." The Conversation, November 13, 2016. https://theconversation.com/central-mali-gripped-by-a-dangerous-brew-of-jihad-revolt-and-self-defence-67668.

"Guinea: Stadium Massacre, Rape Likely Crimes Against Humanity." Human Rights Watch. Human Rights Watch, December 17, 2009. https://www.hrw.org/news/2009/12/17/guinea-stadium-massacre-rape-likely-crimes-against-humanity.

"Herdsmen Killings: Buhari Dey Sleep on Top Bicycle- Wole Soyinka." BBC News Pidgin. BBC, February 13, 2018. https://www.bbc.com/pidgin/tori-43041267.

"Indigenous Peoples, Indigneous Peoples: Factsheet." United Nations Permanent Forum on Indigenous Issues. Accessed July 12, 2020. https://www.un.org/esa/socdev/unpfii/documents/5session_factsheet1.pdf.

Jeune Afrique. "Mali: Le Nouveau Gouvernement De Boubou Cissé Dévoilé – Jeune Afrique," May 5, 2019. https://www.jeuneafrique.com/771068/politique/mali-le-nouveau-gouvernement-de-boubou-cisse-devoile/.

Ka, Racky. "Menace(s) Du Stéréotype Et Perception De Soi: Comment Modérer l'Impact Des Réputations Négatives Sur Les Membres Des Groupes Stéréotypés ? Le Cas Des Femmes Et Des Noirs De France," 2013.

Kaës, René. *Différences Culturelles Et Souffrances De L'identité*. Paris: Dunod, 2005.

Kaës, René. *L'appareil Psychique Groupal Constructions Du Groupe*. Paris: Dunod, 1976.

Kaës, René. *Transmission De La Vie Psychique Entre Générations*. Paris: Dunod, 2013.

Kane, Oumar. *La Première Hégémonie Peule: Le Fuuta Tooro De Koli Tenella à Almaami Abdu*. Paris: Karthala, 2005.

Kéita, Jean Djigui. *Les Mandingues: De Koumbi à Paris*. Bamako: Editions Donniya, 2011.

Konaré, Alpha Oumar, and Adam Ba Konaré. *Grandes Dates Du Mali*. Bamako: Imprimeries du Mali, 1983.

Konaré, Dougoukolo Alpha Oumar. "Transmission Transgénérationnelle Et Identité Ethnique: Clinique Des Peuls d'Afrique Occidentale," 2010.

Koné, Fahiraman Rodrigue. "Centre FrancoPaix En Résolution Des Confits Et Missions De Paix." Centre FrancoPaix, June 2018. https://dandurand.uqam.ca/wp-content/uploads/2018/06/2018_06_Rapport-Kone_CFP_Compresse.pdf.

Kyburz, Olivier. "La Fabrication De La Foulanité." *Journal des africanistes* 67, no. 2 (1997): 101–26.

Kyburz, Olivier. "Les hiérarchies Sociales Et Leurs Fondements idéologiques Chez Les Haalpulaar'en (Sénégal)," 1994.

"La Situation Sécuritaire Au Nord En Débat Sur TV5: Chaudes Empoignades Entre Chato Et Moussa Ag Assarid." Bamadanet, December 17, 2012. http://bamada.net/la-situation-securitaire-au-nord-en-debat-sur-tv5-chaudes-empoignades-entre-chato-et-moussa-ag-assarid.

La Vérité. https://Www.maliweb.net/Insecurite/Crise-Au-Nord-Mali-Ahmed-Mohamed-Ag-Hamani-Appelle-a-La-Tenue-Dune-Conference-Verite-Reconciliation-Nationale-54600.html. Maliweb, March 14, 2012.

Lam, Aboubacry Moussa. *De L'origine égyptienne Des Peuls*. Paris: Présence africaine, 2001.

Le Cam, Morgane. "Au Mali, Un Projet De Loi D'entente Nationale Qui Suscite La Controverse." Le Monde.fr. Le Monde, June 8, 2018. https://www.lemonde.fr/af

rique/article/2018/06/08/au-mali-un-projet-de-loi-d-entente-nationale-qui-suscite-la-controverse_5311887_3212.html.

Lecocq, Baz, and Georg Klute. "Tuareg Separatism in Mali." *International Journal: Canada's Journal of Global Policy Analysis* 68, no. 3 (2013): 424–34. https://doi.org/10.1177/0020702013505431.

Lema, Luis. "Le Sanglot D'une Touareg Du Mali." Le Temps. Le Temps SA, April 13, 2012. https://www.letemps.ch/monde/sanglot-dune-touareg-mali.

L'Indicateur du Renouveau. Actualités en temps réel, opinions et nouvelles du Mali, January 8, 2018. https://www.maliweb.net/editorial/linsecurite-residuelle-na-716-morts-mali-2017-2730288.html.

Macé, Célian. "Au Sahel, 'Je N'ai Pas Besoin De Canons Supplémentaires, Mais Il Nous Faut Gagner En Mobilité.'" Libération.fr. Libération, July 9, 2018. http://www.liberation.fr/planete/2018/07/09/au-sahel-je-n-ai-pas-besoin-de-canons-supplementaires-mais-il-nous-faut-gagner-en-mobilite_1665186.

"Mali: Le Premier Ministre Refuse De Démissionner Et Formera Un Gouvernement d'Union Nationale." KOACI, July 29, 2012. http://koaci.com/m/mali-premier-ministre-refuse-demissionner-formera-gouvernement-d%E2%80%99union-nationale-76523-i.html.

Mnlamov. Malijet. January 27, 2013. http://malijet.com/actualite-politique-au-mali/flash-info/62837-le-mnla-devoile-la-liste-de-son-gouvernement.html.

Monteil, Charles. "Réflexions Sur Le Problème Des Peul." *Journal de la Société des Africanistes* 20, no. 2 (1950): 153–92.

N'Diaye, M. "Le Pulaagu Ou Code De Conduite Des Peul, d'Hier à Aujourd'Hui." In *Peuples Du Sénégal.* Paris: Sepia, 1996.

"Niger: Des Peuls Dénoncent Les Incursions Et Exactions D'ex-Rebelles Maliens." RFI. RFI, May 7, 2018. https://www.rfi.fr/fr/afrique/20180507-niger-peuls-denoncent-incursions-exactions-milices-maliennes.

Pondopoulo, Anna. *Les Français Et Les Peuls: Histoire D'une Relation priviliégiée.* Paris: les Indes savantes, 2009.

"Pr Ali Nouhoum Diallo: 'Si J'avais 16 Ou 17 Ans Aujourd'hui, Je Prendrai Les Armes'." niarela. Journal du Mali, May 31, 2018. https://niarela.net/interviews/pr-ali-nouhoum-diallo-si-javais-16-ou-17-ans-aujourdhui-je-prendrai-les-armes.

Raineri, Luca, and Francesco Strazzari. "State, Secession, and Jihad: The Micropolitical Economy of Conflict in Northern Mali." *African Security* 8, no. 4 (2015): 249–71. https://doi.org/10.1080/19392206.2015.1100501.

Rep. *How Much More Blood Must Be Spilled?* Human Rights Watch, February 10, 2020. https://www.hrw.org/report/2020/02/11/how-much-more-blood-must-be-spilled/atrocities-against-civilians-central-mali.

Rep. *Report of the United Nations High Commissioner for Human Rights on the Situation of Human Rights in Mali.* United Nations, January 7, 2013. https://www.ohchr.org/Documents/HRBodies/HRCouncil/RegularSession/Session22/A-HRC-22-33_en.pdf.

Rep. *"We Used to Be Brothers": Self-Defense Group Abuses in Central Mali.* New York City, NY: Human Rights Watch, 2018.

Rfi. "La Minusma Confirme Une Bavure De Militaires Maliens Du G5 Sahel à Boulikessi." RFI. RFI, June 26, 2018. http://www.rfi.fr/fr/afrique/20180627-minusma-bavure-militaires-maliens-g5-sahel-boulikessi.

Rfi. "Mali: Tentative De Conciliation Après Les Affrontements De Douentza." RFI. RFI, June 13, 2016. http://www.rfi.fr/afrique/20160613-mali-tentative-conciliation-apres-affrontements-douentza.

Riesman, Paul. *Freedom in Fulani Social Life: an Introspective Ethnography*. Chicago: University of Chicago Press, 1998.

Robinson, David. *The Holy War of Umar Tal: the Western Sahara in the Mid-Nineteenth Century*. Oxford: Clarendon Press, 1985.

Róheim, Géza, and Roger Dadoun. *Origine Et Fonction De La Culture*. Paris: Gallimard, 1972.

Sanankoua, Bintou. *Un Empire Peul Au XIXe siècle: La Diina Du Maasina*. Paris: Karthala, 1990.

Seydou, Christiane. *Profils De Femmes Dans Les récits épiques Peuls Mali-Niger*. Paris: Éd. Karthala, 2010.

Tounkara, Aly. "Hiérarchisation Ethnique Et Extrémisme Violent Au Centre Du Mali Vers Une Nouvelle Rébellion Dans Un Contexte D'insécurité Généralisée." Contre-discours radical, April 7, 2017. https://cdradical.hypotheses.org/538.

Troup Buchanan, Rose. "The Fourth Most Deadly Terror Group That You've Never Heard Of." The Independent. Independent Digital News and Media, November 18, 2015. https://www.independent.co.uk/news/world/africa/global-terrorism-index-nigerian-fulani-militants-named-as-fourth-deadliest-terror-group-in-world-a6739851.html.

Tyam, Mohammadou Aliou, and Henri Gaden. *La Vie D'El Hadj Omar: Qacida En Poular*. Paris: Institut d'Ethnologie, 1935.

Ursu, Anca-Elena. Rep. *Under the Gun: Resource Conflicts and Embattled Traditional Authorities in Central Mali*, July 2018. https://www.clingendael.org/sites/default/files/2018-07/under-the-gun.pdf.

WHITE, Bruce. "What Percentage of All Conflict Is Caused by Identity?" The Organization for Identity & Cultural Development. OICD, December 30, 2017. https://oicd.net/what-percentage-of-all-conflict-is-caused-by-identity/.

"World Report 2013: Rights Trends in World Report 2013: Mali." Human Rights Watch, February 7, 2013. https://www.hrw.org/world-report/2013/country-chapters/mali.

Wout, Daryl, Henry Danso, James Jackson, and Steve Spencer. "The Many Faces of Stereotype Threat: Group- and Self-Threat." *Journal of Experimental Social Psychology* 44, no. 3 (2008): 792–99. https://doi.org/10.1016/j.jesp.2007.07.005.

Index

Aguelhok, 55
Algiers Agreements, 37, 51, 80
Aliou Nouhoum Diallo, 70, 77–79, 83
Alpha Condé, 68
Amadou Aya Sanogo, 39
Amadou Kouffa, 79, 81
Amadou Toumani Touré, 23, 32
Ansar Dine, 55, 79
Anti-Fula racism, 67–69
Anti-Tamasheq Sentiment, 36
Arab Movement of Azawad (MAA), 56
Army of Mali, 40, 76
Azawad, 40, 51, 52, 57

Bazoumana Sissoko, 31
Bozo, 32, 49, 53, 56, 85

castes, 19, 21, 22, 32, 73, 76, 79
CELHTO, 26
Cellou Dalein Diallo, 70, 79
Chapter VII, 1
Cheick Modibo Diarra, 42
clinical psychology, 11
Coordination of Movements and Patriotic Resistance Front (CMFPR), 82
Coup d'État of March 2012 in Mali, 39–41, 54

Dawsahak, 56, 58

demobilization, disarmament, and reintegration (DDR), 80, 81
Dogon, 13, 19, 20, 21, 77; Dogon Country, 20, 49, 50, 83; Dogon Diaspora, 20
Douentza, 66, 77–79
Dozo, 73, 74

Fatoumata Dicko, 66, 76–78
Federation of Mali, 38
Firhoun Ag Alinsar, 36
French colonization, 2, 23, 67
Fula Archipelago, 6, 66
Fula Genocide, 71
Fula racism, 49, 67

G5 Sahel, 57
Gacce, 64
Ganda Izo, 82
Ganda Koy, 82
gender, 76, 77
griot, 21, 22, 26, 33, 34
group psychology, 13
Guinea, 67–69

Hamma Founé Diallo, 81, 82
Harouna Toureh, 80
High Council for the Unity of Azawad (HCUA), 56

human rights, 8, 77
Humbeɓe, 49

Ibrahim Boubacar Keita, 31, 32, 37, 80
Information and Communications Technology (ICT), 47; Facebook, 47, 50, 76; Signal, 48; Social media, 55, 70; WhatsApp, 15, 47, 48, 50, 67
Islamic State in the Greater Sahara (ISGS), 57
Ismaila Cissé, 78, 81–83
Iyad Ag Ghal, 55

Jelgooji, 12
Jihadists, 73, 74, 79–81

Katiba Macina, 79
Kisal, 8, 77
Kurukan Fuga, 25–27

Lenyol Gootol, Demngal Gootal, 15, 65
Léopold Sédar Senghor, 38, 39
Libya, 52, 54, 55

Macina Kingdom, 6, 20, 22
Mahamadou Dieri Maïga, 56
Mande, 32, 92; Charter of Mande, 25–27; Epic of Mande, 24–26; Grand Mali, 36, 66; Great Mande, 20, 34, 36, 92
MNA, 52
Modibo Keita, 38, 39
Mohamed El Moctar, 80
Moussa Ag Acharatoumane, 52, 56, 57
Moussa Ag Asarid, 41
Moussa Traoré, 31
Movement for Oneness and Jihad in West Africa (MUJWA), 6, 55, 72, 77, 78, 85
Movement for the Defense of the Fatherland (MDP), 81

Movement for the Salvation of Azawad (MSA), 56–58

National Movement for the Liberation of Azawad (MNLA), 6, 40, 51, 53, 54, 56, 81, 82, 92
Nigeria, 71, 72

Opération Barkhane, 57, 58
Opération Serval, 66

Pan-Fulaness, 15, 16, 71, 92
Pax Mali, 23, 92
Pulaaku, 63, 64, 67, 92

racial anthropology, 67, 69
Radio Seno, 49
Resolution 2100, 1

Sebɓe, 49
Sékou Touré, 67–69
Self-Defense Group of Imghad Tamasheq and Allies (GATIA), 82
Sénégal, 38, 39
social memory, 49
Sunjata, 25, 31, 33, 49

Tabital Pulaaku, 49, 65, 66, 81
Tamasheq rebellion, 6, 34, 37, 40, 51
Tarikh Al Fattash, 22
Tarikh Al Sudan, 22

Umarian Jihad, 34, 35
United Nations, 1
United Nations Education, Science, and Culture Organization (UNESCO), 26
United Nations Multidimensional Integrated Stabilization Mission in Mali (MINUSMA), 3, 4, 37

About the Author

Dougoukolo Alpha Oumar Ba Konaré is a clinical psychologist. He teaches about Fula civilization at France's Institut National des Langues et Civilisations Orientales. He has been working on religious experiences, intercultural psychology, human rights and conflicts in the Sahel, and identity in the Fula nation. Dougoukolo obtained his doctorate on "The Functions of Religious Investment: Study of a Malian Muslim Population" from Paris Descartes University (France) in 2013. In 2017, he completed a master's degree in strategic studies and defense policies. In addition to his academic activities, he is an activist in associations promoting human rights, youths, women, and minorities. He is a founding member of Kisal, a human rights organization working with communities from the Sahel.

CPSIA information can be obtained
at www.ICGtesting.com
Printed in the USA
BVHW031413160421
605144BV00001B/54